Preface

I0032306

    The tens of thousands of wars and conflicts in history, and the perennial incompetency, imposed widespread poverty and suffering on the planet. Now all people want to immediately change this unacceptable situation, and start a new and better life, based on peace, no arms, freedom, good health, good education, good jobs, harmony and prosperity for all on our beloved Earth!

    Why these perennial war errors persisted for so long? There are many fundamental questions that all human beings are called to answer. The most important philosophers, including Socrates, Plato, Aristotle, Descartes, and Kant, always asked profound questions, and gave eternal answers.

    This book presents many examples from history, clearly showing how bad the wars and incompetence are, stopping or even reversing the advancement of our civilization, and comparing with new ideas, which will create the conditions for a peaceful, free, healthy, harmonious and prosperous life for all on our Peaceful Terra.

    The future begins to take shape in front of our eyes, and is amazingly attractive!

Michael M. Dediu, Ph. D.

Nashua, New Hampshire, U. S. A., 11 July 2021

On West 42nd Street at Fifth Avenue, looking southeast at Chrysler building (back up, Walter P. Chrysler (1875-1940), 1930, 319 m, 77 floors, 111,000 m^2 floor area, 32 elevators, at Lexington Avenue), before it is Grand Hyatt New York Hotel (1919, 90 m), and before it is Grand Central Terminal (1871, 1903, 1913, 2000, built by Cornelius Vanderbilt (1794-1877, the 2nd richest American, after John D. Rockefeller (1839-1937)) and his 13 children, commuter railroad terminal, with a grand façade and concourse, at Park Avenue, 47 acres, 44 high-level platforms, 67 tracks on 2 levels).

Table of Contents

France, Paris, Musée du Louvre (1793, in Palais du Louvre (1550)):
from Cour Napoléon (between 1862-1867 Napoléon III reunited les
Tuileries au Louvre), the right side of the central part of the western
façade of Pavillon de l'Horloge or Pavillon Sully (1624 – 1654,
under Kings Louis XIII (1601 – 1643, reign 1610 – 1643), and Louis
XIV (1638 – 1715, reign 1643 – 1715)), which is on the east side of
Cour Napoléon and of the west side of Cour Carrée.

Question 1. When did people invent languages?

Response 1. Circa 300,000 years ago the languages were invented by people isolated in small groups in different parts of the planet. Languages are a sine qua non requirement for the development of the civilization.

Unfortunately, people also started wars, which immediately created difficulties for everyone to prosper.

They should have started to think about living in peace and harmony – but they didn't, therefore we did, and created the new Constitution of the World, whose objective is simply to help all the people on Earth to live better, peacefully, free, healthy, harmoniously, and prosperously.

More precisely, the Constitution starts with 7 details about its objectives:

We, the People on this Earth, in order to

1.1 - completely eliminate war and any type of conflicts,

1.2 - have a peaceful and harmonious world,

1.3 - have freedom, dignity, good families and respect,

1.4 - have good health and good education,

1.5 - have a friendly atmosphere and prosperity,

1.6 – have the safety and wellbeing of all the people in the world as the highest priority,

1.7 – use the best peaceful results, experience and knowledge of all current countries,

establish this Constitution of the World.

Italy, Venezia, Libreria Sansoviniana (left), Il Campanile (center-left), Palazzo Ducale (right), and a Japanese couple wedding picture.

Question 2. When and where did the quantification of time start?

Response 2. Probably around 20000 BC, in the current territory of France – these are the earliest known prehistoric attempts to quantify time, which is very important, because everything is a function of time (number 20 in Bibliography).

At that time people did not know that time is money, and they wasted time on wars – now people know that peace is the first priority – without peace not much can be done.

Italy, Roma: On Ponte Palatino (1891), the remaining arch of the Pons Aemilius (178 BC, Ponte Rotto, left), Pons Fabricius (62 BC, right).

Question 3. When did people invent the numeral system?

Response 3. Around 3400 BC, in Mesopotamia, the Sumerians invented the first numeral system, and a system of weights and measures – smart people, they could have begun to think that all the people of the world are proud citizens of only one country.

Now we call it Peaceful Terra, with total area of over 509 M km^2, and land area over 148 M km^2.

Being just one country, there are no borders, therefore no conflicts, no wars!

USA, Boston, 3 Dec 2009, from Avenue Louis Pasteur (1822-1895, French microbiologist), Boston Public Latin School (1635, Schola Latina Bostoniensis, the oldest and the first public exam school in the U.S.).

Question 4. When was the Sumerian cuneiform writing invented?

Response 4. Around 3200 BC the Sumerian cuneiform writing system was invented, which helped to begin to describe some scientific work.

Unfortunately, it was also used to write more and more rules – they did not think to limit the number of rules.

But now - not too many rules is much better:

All the rules – not more than 2,000, on maximum 1,000 pages - on our Earth will be established by the people and their elected Advisers.

All rules proposed by Advisers must be approved by their 5 assistants (doctors, mathematicians, CEOs, engineers and teachers), and for any new rule over 2,000 basic rules (each rule on at most half a page, total 1,000 pages), at least on old rule must be eliminated.

All the rules can be changed or eliminated when a majority of the people or their Advisors agree, but some fundamental peace and order rules will remain.

Question 5. When did the administration of a territory appear?

Response 5. Around 3150 BC the first dynasty of Egypt begins, and the rulers had some specialized people around, who were working on the administration of Egypt – this is also the start of bureaucracy.

Now, Peaceful Terra, being a very big country, will be divided in 10 simple regions:

For easier administration, Peaceful Terra will be only administratively divided in 10 simple and friendly regions of around 770 M people each, called R0, R1,…, R9, which will be delimited by meridians (or line of longitudes), with the assistance of the United Nations.

A south-west view of Rome from Altare della Patria: Theatrum Marcelli (the Theatre of Marcellus (Marcus Claudius Marcellus, 42 BC – 23 BC, Emperor Augustus' nephew), 13 BC, left back).

Question 6. When was the decimal system invented?

Response 6. Around 3100 BC, in Egypt, the earliest known decimal system appears. Very important, but they were busy with war errors, instead of beginning to think where the capitals should be located.

The capital can be everywhere! Because the capitals tend to become huge bureaucracies, with lots of people trying to be there, without much usefulness, Peaceful Terra will have moving capitals, to benefit everybody.

Each region will have a pair of capitals plus an outside city, for better and more homogenous management (all will change every year; more details are in the annex book "World with One Country & its Ten Friendly Regions - Moving from 195 disagreeing countries, to 1 country with 10 collaborating regions"). For example, the first implementation will be:
R0 between meridians 0 and 15^0 E, capitals: Bern (Switzerland), Libreville (Gabon), and Oxford (UK).
R1: 15^0 E - 30^0 E, Warsaw (Poland), Pretoria (South Africa) and Miami (FL, USA).
R2: 30^0 E - 45^0 E, Moscow (Russia), Cairo (Egypt), and Grenoble (France).
R3: 45^0 E - 75^0 E, Astana (Kazakhstan), Karachi (Pakistan), and Montpellier (France).
R4: 75^0 E - 85^0 E, New Delhi (India), Novosibirsk (Russia), and Magdeburg (Germany).
R5: 85^0 E - 100^0 E, Krasnoyarsk (Russia), Urumqi (China), and Avignon (France).
R6: 100^0 E - 115^0 E, Jakarta (Indonesia), Beijing (China), and Neuchâtel (Switzerland).
R7: 115^0 E - 180^0, Tokyo (Japan), Sydney (Australia), and Malmö (Sweden).

R8: 180^0 - 70^0 Washington (USA), Mexico City (Mexico), and Bellinzona (Switzerland).

R9: 70^0 W – 0 Halifax (Canada), Brasilia (Brazil), and Biel (Switzerland).

Japan, Nikko, (140 km north of Tokyo): Toshogu Shrine, Japan's most lavishly decorated shrine, and the mausoleum of Tokugawa Ieyasu, the founder of the Tokugawa shogunate (1600-1850).

In the first implementation, there are many big differences between the populations of different regions, and then between the populations of different sub-regions, but this is just the first implementation, which needs to be quickly put in place, and then, very easily, the delimitations will be moved a few kilometers east or west, to reach a balanced population.

Because all the people are in the same country, it is normal to modify a little its regions, for better administration, to make everybody happy.

It is well understood that there will be some difficulties in the beginning, like in all beginnings, but with calm, patience, perseverance and hard work, the things will improve fast, and all the people will enjoy a better life.

Rome (753 BC), Vatican (1929): Piazza di San Pietro (1656 – 1667, Bernini), with Moderno's façade (115 m wide, 46 m high) of the Basilica di San Pietro (1506 – 1626), and an Egyptian obelisk.

Question 7. We all have a calendar – when did it start?

Response 7. Around 3000 BC the Egyptian calendar with 360 days was introduced, based on studies of mathematicians and astronomers. Great discovery, but, again, instead of using the calendars for planning ahead for the future regions and sub-regions, they lost everything with bad war mistakes.

Each of the 10 regions will be divided by meridians in 10 sub-regions S00, , S99, each with about 77 M people.

Then each of the 100 sub-regions will be divided in 10 districts:

Each of the 100 sub-regions will be divided in 10 districts D000, D001, , D999, each with about 7.7 M people, and each of the districts will have their current small and big cities.

All these delimitations between regions, as well as between sub-regions, will be flexible:

There will be just simple administrative delimitations, and all these delimitations between regions, as well as between sub-regions, will be flexible – they will be changed after each census (5 years), for maintaining a balanced number of people in all regions (around 770 M) and sub-regions (around 77 M).

Question 8. There are many big cities now – when the first major city appeared?

Response 8: Around 2700 BC Minoan civilization ancient palace city Knossos (on the north of the central part of the Greek island Crete, 340 km southeast of Athens) reached 80,000 inhabitants, some of them working on good ideas. The first settlement was in about 7000 BC.

The Old Kingdom begins in Egypt, and will support many useful works, but all was lost because pf the war mistakes.

Meridians are easy to use, impartial, helpful for people with telework:

Having telework, many people will have a northern residence and a southern residence, seasonally moving from one to the other, to avoid extreme cold or heat, and having the same hour.

Question 9. Plenty of literature now – when did it start?

Response 9: From around 2600 BC there is the oldest known surviving literature: Sumerian texts from Abu Salabikh, including the Instructions of Shuruppak and the Kesh temple hymn. Sumer is the earliest known civilization in the historical region of southern Mesopotamia, between the Tigris and Euphrates rivers, in the area that later became Babylonia, and is now southern Iraq, from around Baghdad to the Persian Gulf, emerging during the early Bronze Ages, around 4500 BC, and continuing for about 2600 years, until circa 1900 BC. Many useful Sumerian discoveries are lost because of the war errors.

Harmony is essential - all the oceans will belong to some of the regions, and working harmoniously to maintain and clean the oceans will give beautiful results:

All the oceans will belong to some of the regions defined above, therefore will be maintained by those regions, to be free of any piracy or other bad activity – World Police will help when necessary.

The harmony will generate strong cooperation for the maintenance of the oceans, which will also become residence for many people.

Question 10. We all admire the Great Pyramid of Giza – when was completed?

Response 10: In 2560 BC, during Pharaoh Khufu, the Great Pyramid of Giza, 146.5 m, was completed – great engineering achievement. Also, 440 years after the incomplete Egyptian calendar with 360 days was introduced, this Egyptian pyramid of Cheops (the Greek name of Khufu) at Gizeh, near Cairo, included a tablet recording mythical explanations given by the priests, of the extra five days added to the Egyptian calendar of 360 days, but in fact the extra 5 days were re-calculated by mathematicians and astronomers, based on practical observations over 4 centuries. In this way, the 365 days calendar was introduced, and, after over 4,580 years, with some small corrections, it is still used today – imagine how many other significant discoveries would be available today, if the wars wouldn't have destroyed them!

The family of over 7. 7 B people from Peaceful Terra will have four levels of world management; at the local level, if needed, it could be one or two more levels of local managers (mayors, town managers, county managers – all levels of management must be friendly, helpful, fast, polite, modest and smart):

Level 1 Management: 1,000 L1 friendly managers, for the 1,000 districts, who will supervise and assist the mayors and town managers from their district, for a total of about 7,700,000 people in each district. Each of the 1,000 L1 friendly managers will be located in a central city from their districts – they could be the mayors of those cities, but with new responsibilities for the whole district.

Level 2 Management: 100 L2 friendly managers, for the 100 sub-regions, who will supervise and assist the 10 L1 managers of the 10 districts of each sub-region, for a total of about 77,000,000 people for each sub-region. These 100 L2 friendly managers will move each month between the two capitals of each of the 100 sub-regions.

Italy, Cividale del Friuli, 3 Nov 2009, on Largo Boiani, looking northeast to il Duomo di Santa Maria Assunta (1457-1529, center left), Campanile (center right up), a statue down of Giulio Caesare (100 BC – 44 BC), signs to right to Castelmonte 9 km, and Gorizia 28 km.

Question 11. When was the precise astronomical calendar created?

Response 11: Around 2400 BC, In Egypt, the precise astronomical calendar was created, and it was used for over 3,500 years, even in the Middle Ages, for its mathematical regularity – very impressive achievement; many others were destroyed by wars, delaying the advancement of the civilization.

Discussing with people in a harmonious atmosphere and understanding each other, will certainly help to choose, in the beginning, these capitals:

In Region R0: from Paris (France) to N'Djamena (Chad)

- The sub-region R00 will have the capitals Paris (France) and Niamey (Niger) – assistance from Magdeburg (Germany).
- The sub-region R01 will have the capitals Brussels (Belgium) and Porto-Novo (Benin) - assistance from Toronto (Canada).
- The sub-region R02 will have the capitals Amsterdam (Netherlands) and Algiers (Algeria) - assistance from Graz (Austria).
- The sub-region R03 will have the capitals Luxembourg (Luxembourg) and Sao Tome (Sao Tome and Principe) - assistance from Adelaide (Australia).
- The sub-region R04 will have the capitals of Abuja (Nigeria) and Bochum (Germany) - assistance from Nikko (Japan).
- The sub-region R05 will have the capitals Malabo (Equatorial Guinea), and Zürich (Switzerland) - assistance from Leeds (UK).
- The sub-region R06 will have the capitals Oslo (Norway) and Tunis (Tunisia) - assistance from Sheffield (UK).
- The sub-region R07 will have the capitals Roma (Italy) and Luanda (Angola) - assistance from Yamagata (Japan).

- The sub-region R08 will have the capitals in Berlin (Germany) and Tripoli (Libya) - assistance from New York (USA).
- The sub-region R09 will have the capitals Prague (Czech Republic) and N'Djamena (Chad) - assistance from Brisbane (Australia).

Japan, Inzai: A blooming tree (left) in the mid of November 2008, near an artesian fountain in the central park from the Inzai (Chiba) campus of Tokyo Denki University, at sunset.

In Region R1: from Zagreb (Croatia) to Bujumbura (Burundi)

- The sub-region R10 will have the capitals in Zagreb (Croatia) and Brazzaville (Congo) - assistance from Nantes (France).
- The sub-region R11 will have the capitals in Vienna (Austria), Windhoek (Namibia) - assistance from Bilbao (Spain).
- The sub-region R12 will have the capitals in Stockholm (Sweden), Bangui (Central African Republic) - assistance from Florence (Italy).
- The sub-region R13 will have the capitals in Budapest (Hungary), Rundu (Namibia) - assistance from Monaco (Monaco).
- The sub-region R14 will have the capitals in Belgrade (Serbia), Kananga (Democratic Republic of Congo) - assistance from Liverpool (UK).
- The sub-region R15 will have the capitals in Athens (Greece), Mongu (Zambia) - assistance from Los Angeles (CA, USA).
- The sub-region R16 will have the capitals in Helsinki (Finland) and Kolwezi (Democratic Republic of the Congo) - assistance from Montreal (Canada).
- The sub-region R17 will have the capitals in Bucharest (Romania) and Gaborone (Botswana) - assistance from Philadelphia (PA, USA).
- The sub-region R18 will have the capitals in Minsk (Belarus) and Maseru (Lesotho) - assistance from Orleans (France).
- The sub-region R19 will have the capitals in Chisinau (Republic of Moldova) and Bujumbura (Burundi) - assistance from Hamburg (Germany).

Italy, 6 April 1978, Pisa, Palazzo della Carovana (1562-1564) now for Scuola Normale Superiore (1810, by Napoleon Bonaparte (1769-1821), 460 students, 6% admission rate, best in Italy).

In Region R2: from Kiev (Ukraine) to Baghdad (Iraq)

- The sub-region R20 will have the capitals in Kiev (Ukraine) and Kigali (Rwanda) - assistance from Ottawa (Canada).
- The sub-region R21 will have the capitals in Ankara (Turkey) and Khartoum (Sudan) - assistance from Salzburg (Austria).
- The sub-region R22 will have the capitals in Lilongwe (Malawi) and Nicosia (Cyprus) - assistance from Dallas (TX, USA).
- The sub-region R23 will have the capitals in Jerusalem (Israel) and Dodoma (Tanzania) - assistance from Strasbourg (France).
- The sub-region R24 will have the capitals in Damascus (Syria) and Nairobi (Kenya) - assistance from Stuttgart (Germany).
- The sub-region R25 will have the capitals in Krasnodar (Russia) and Addis Ababa (Ethiopia) - assistance from Marseille (France).
- The sub-region R26 will have the capitals in Rostov-on-Don (Russia) and Asmara (Eritrea) - assistance from Leipzig (Germany).
- The sub-region R27 will have the capitals in Stavropol (Russia) and Djibouti (Djibouti) - assistance from Zürich (Switzerland).
- The sub-region R28 will have the capitals in Mosul (Iraq) and Moroni (Comoros) - assistance from Linz (Austria).
- The sub-region R29 will have the capitals in Yerevan (Armenia) and Baghdad (Iraq) - assistance from Göttingen (Germany).

Italy, Roma, the south and east sides of the Arch (315) of Constantine (272 – 337, Roman Emperor 306 - 337), from Via di San Gregorio

In Region R3: from Riyadh (Saudi Arabia) to Malé (Maldives)

- The sub-region R30 will have the capitals in Riyadh (Saudi Arabia) and Mogadishu (Somalia) - assistance from Bonn (Germany).
- The sub-region R31 will have the capitals in Baku (Azerbaijan) and Antananarivo (Madagascar) - assistance from Le Mans (France).
- The sub-region R32 will have the capitals in Oral (Kazakhstan) and Tehran (Iran) - assistance from Pisa (Italy).
- The sub-region R33 will have the capitals in Ashgabat (Turkmenistan) and Abu Dhabi (United Arab Emirates) - assistance from Wolfsburg (Germany).
- The sub-region R34 will have the capitals in Magnitogorsk (Russia) and Muscat (Oman) - assistance from Toulouse (France).
- The sub-region R35 will have the capitals in Chelyabinsk (Russia) and Herat (Afghanistan) - assistance from Basel (Switzerland).
- The sub-region R36 will have the capitals in Tyumen (Russia) and Kandahar (Afghanistan) - assistance from Nagoya (Japan).
- The sub-region R37 will have the capitals in Dushanbe (Tajikistan) and Labytnangi (Russia) - assistance from Limoges (France).
- The sub-region R38 will have the capitals in Tashkent (Uzbekistan) and Kabul (Afghanistan) - assistance from Rostock (Germany).
- The sub-region R39 will have the capitals in Islamabad (Pakistan) and Malé (Maldives) - assistance from La Rochelle (France).

Italy, Roma, Temple of Saturn (42 BC, left up), Curia (283, center-left up), Nerva's Forum (97, down), Nerva 30 - 98, Emperor 96 – 98).

In Region R4: from Bishkek (Kyrgyzstan) to Brahmapur (India)

- The sub-region R40 will have the capitals in Bishkek (Kyrgyzstan) and Jaipur (India) - assistance from Osaka (Japan).
- The sub-region R41 will have the capitals in Akola (India) and Kashgar (China) - assistance from Genoa (Italy).
- The sub-region R42 will have the capitals in Almaty (Kazakhstan) and Coimbatore (India) - assistance from Perth (Australia).
- The sub-region R43 will have the capitals in Kuybyshev (Russia) and Agra (India) - assistance from Fukuoka (Japan).
- The sub-region R44 will have the capitals in Vertikos (Russia) and Nagpur (India) - assistance from Coral Bay (Australia).
- The sub-region R45 will have the capitals in Chennai (India) and Colombo (Sri Lanka) - assistance from Sapporo (Japan).
- The sub-region R46 will have the capitals in Lucknow (India) and Fedosikha (Russia) - assistance from Niigata (Japan).
- The sub-region R47 will have the capitals in Bilaspur (India) and Kolpashevo (Russia) - assistance from Albany (Australia).
- The sub-region R48 will have the capitals in Visakhapatnam (India) and Barnaul (Russia) - assistance from Hiroshima (Japan).
- The sub-region R49 will have the capitals in Brahmapur (India) and Tomsk (Russia) - assistance from Yokohama (Japan).

In Region R5: from Kathmandu (Nepal) to Dehong (China)

- The sub-region R50 will have the capitals in Kathmandu (Nepal) and Patna (India) - assistance from Kobe (Japan).
- The sub-region R51 will have the capitals in Bayingol (China) and Novokuznetsk (Russia) - assistance from Vichy (France).
- The sub-region R52 will have the capitals in Thimphu (Bhutan) and Dhaka (Bangladesh) - assistance from Jena (Germany).
- The sub-region R53 will have the capitals in Lhasa (China) and Achinsk (Russia) - assistance from Reims (France).
- The sub-region R54 will have the capitals in Abakan (Russia) and Kumul (China) - assistance from Fribourg (Switzerland).
- The sub-region R55 will have the capitals in Kyzyl (Russia) and Dibrugarh (India) - assistance from Denmark (Australia).
- The sub-region R56 will have the capitals in Bassein (Myanmar) and Tinsukia (India) - assistance from Chiba (Japan).
- The sub-region R57 will have the capitals in Yushu City (China) and Tinskoy (Russia) - assistance from Klagenfurt (Austria).
- The sub-region R58 will have the capitals in Jiuquan (China) and Medan (Indonesia) - assistance from Lucerne (Switzerland).
- The sub-region R59 will have the capitals in Chiang Mai (Thailand) and Dehong (China) - assistance from Mulhouse (France).

Italy, Rome: The Temple of Vesta and Rome and a flag throwing festival on 8 December 2011

In Region R6: from Bangkok (Thailand) to Chita (Russia)

- The sub-region R60 will have the capitals in Bangkok (Thailand) and Kuala Lumpur (Malaysia) - assistance from Besançon (France).
- The sub-region R61 will have the capitals in Vientiane (Laos) and Singapore – assistance from Freiburg im Breisgau (Germany).
- The sub-region R62 will have the capitals in Phnom Penh (Cambodia) and Irkutsk (Russia) – assistance from Baden (Switzerland).
- The sub-region R63 will have the capitals in Palembang (Indonesia), Hanoi (Vietnam) – assistance from Thun (Switzerland).
- The sub-region R64 will have the capitals in Ulan Bator (Mongolia) and Ulan-Ude (Russia) – assistance from Chaumont (France).
- The sub-region R65 will have the capitals in Cirebon (Indonesia) and Nanning (China) – assistance from Vaduz (Lichtenstein).
- The sub-region R66 will have the capitals in Pontianak (Indonesia) and Baotou (China) – assistance from Lugano (Switzerland).
- The sub-region R67 will have the capitals in Surakarta (Indonesia) and Yichang (China) – assistance from Thonon-les-Bain (France).
- The sub-region R68 will have the capitals in Surabaya (Indonesia) and Changsha (China) – assistance from Burgdorf (Switzerland).
- The sub-region R69 will have the capitals in Chita (Russia) and Hong Kong (China) – assistance from Colmar (France).

Japan, Tokyo, In Shinjuku, from the 45th fl., 202 m, of Tokyo Met. Gov Bldg.: KDDI Bldg. (165 m, 32 fl, 1974, center), NTT Docomo Yoyogi Bldg. (240 m, 27 fl, 2000, Shibuya, center up), Yoyogi Park (right).

In Region R7: from Nanchang (China) to Melbourne (Australia)

- The sub-region R70 will have the capitals in Bandar Seri Begawan (Brunei Darussalam) and Nanchang (China) – assistance from Turku (Finland).
- The sub-region R71 will have the capitals in Krasnokamensk (Russia) and Jinan (China) – assistance from St. Gallen (Switzerland).
- The sub-region R72 will have the capitals in Baguio City (Philippines) and Hangzhou (China) – assistance from Dole (France).
- The sub-region R73 will have the capitals in Manila (Philippines) and Taipei (Taiwan, China) – assistance from Metz (France).
- The sub-region R74 will have the capitals in Kupang (Indonesia) and Shanghai (China) – assistance from Davos (Switzerland).
- The sub-region R75 will have the capitals in Pyongyang (North Korea) and Seoul (South Korea) – assistance from Versailles (France).
- The sub-region R76 will have the capitals in Vladivostok (Russia) and Busan (South Korea) – assistance from Innsbruck (Austria).
- The sub-region R77 will have the capitals in Kyoto (Japan) and Khabarovsk (Russia) – assistance from Germering (Germany).
- The sub-region R78 will have the capitals in Nagoya (Japan) and Komsomolsk-on-Amur (Russia) – assistance from Venice (Italy).
- The sub-region R79 will have the capitals in Sendai (Japan) and Melbourne (Australia) – assistance from St. Moritz (Switzerland).

France, Paris, the north-west part of L'Institut de France (1795, moved in 1805 by Napoléon in this baroque building from 1684) is a revered French cultural society with five académies, the most famous being Académie Français (1635) and. Académie des sciences (1666).

In Region R8: from Anchorage (Alaska, USA) to Lima (Peru)

- The sub-region R80 will have the capitals in Uelen (Russia) and Anchorage (Alaska, USA), – assistance from Zug (Switzerland).
- The sub-region R81 will have the capitals in Vancouver (Canada) and San Jose (CA, USA) – assistance from Odense (Denmark).
- The sub-region R82 will have the capitals in Vernon (Canada) and Los Angeles (CA, USA) – assistance from Amstetten (Austria).
- The sub-region R83 will have the capitals in Calgary (Canada) and Tijuana (Mexico) – assistance from Chur (Switzerland).
- The sub-region R84 will have the capitals in Hermosillo (Mexico) and Tucson (AR, USA) – assistance from Bergen (Norway).
- The sub-region R85 will have the capitals in Chihuahua (Mexico) and Regina (Canada) – assistance from Gothenburg (Sweden).
- The sub-region R86 will have the capitals in San Luis Potosi City (Mexico) and Winnipeg (Canada) – assistance from Yverdon-les-Bains (Switzerland).
- The sub-region R87 will have the capitals in Tulsa (OK, USA) and Veracruz (Mexico) – assistance from Bregenz (Austria).
- The sub-region R88 will have the capitals in Memphis (TN, USA) and San José (Costa Rica) – assistance from Uppsala (Sweden).
- The sub-region R89 will have the capitals in Lima (Peru) and Boston (MA, USA) – assistance from Tampere (Finland).

UK, London, Greenwich: Looking northwest to the southeast side of the South Building (1899, Astronomy Center) of Royal Observatory Greenwich (1676).

In Region R9: from La Paz (Bolivia) to London (United Kingdom)

- The sub-region R90 will have the capitals in La Paz (Bolivia) and Bangor (Maine, USA) – assistance from Aosta (Italy).
- The sub-region R91 will have the capitals in Caracas (Venezuela) and Road Town (British Virgin Islands) – assistance from Obergoms (Switzerland).
- The sub-region R92 will have the capitals in Buenos Aires (Argentina) and Fort-de-France (Martinique) – assistance from Freudenstadt (Germany).
- The sub-region R93 will have the capitals in Asuncion (Paraguay) and Montevideo (Uruguay) – assistance from Winterthur (Switzerland).
- The sub-region R94 will have the capitals in Cayenne (French Guiana), St. John's (Canada) – assistance from Novara (Italy).
- The sub-region R95 will have the capitals in Rio de Janeiro (Brazil) and Dakar (Senegal) – assistance from Toyama (Japan).
- The sub-region R96 will have the capitals in Freetown (Sierra Leone) and Lisbon (Portugal) – assistance from Kawasaki (Japan).
- The sub-region R97 will have the capitals in Bamako (Mali) and Athlone (Ireland) – assistance from Ulm (Germany).
- The sub-region R98 will have the capitals in Yamoussoukro (Cote d'Ivoire) and Madrid (Spain) – assistance from Okayama (Japan).
- The sub-region R99 will have the capitals in Ouagadougou (Burkina Faso) and London (United Kingdom) - assistance from Vaasa (Finland).

Italy, Roma: Arch of Severus (203, center-right), Temple of Saturn (42 BC, center), Temple of Vespasian (80, left).

Question 12. What number base was used in Babylonia?

Response 12: Around 2000 BC in Mesopotamia, the Babylonians used a sexagesimal or base-60 number system, and is still used, with modifications, for measuring time, angles, and geographic coordinates. They also computed the first known approximate value of π at 3.125 – pretty close to the correct value of 3.141592…..

Many other great discoveries were lost because of war errors – they could have helped with the level 3 management, for example.

Level 3 Management: Ten L3 friendly managers for the 10 regions, who will supervise and assist the 10 L2 managers of the 10 sub-regions of each region, for a total of about 770,000,000 people for each region.

- The Region R0 will have the first capitals in

Bern (Switzerland) and Libreville (Gabon) – assistance from Oxford (UK).

For better quality and consistency of the management, we'll have the first two cities from the region R0, and the third city from outside. Actually, being inside the same country Terra, any city, sub-region or region can ask for advice or help from anybody.

- The Region R1 will have the first capitals in

Warsaw (Poland) and Pretoria (South Africa) – assistance from Miami (FL, USA).

- The Region R2 will have the first capitals in

Moscow (Russia) and Cairo (Egypt) – assistance from Grenoble (France).

- The Region R3 will have the first capitals in

Astana (Kazakhstan) and Karachi (Pakistan), – assistance from Montpellier (France).

UK, Cambridge, a bas-relief on the eastern wall of the western building of the Old Court (1451) of Queens' College (1448), University of Cambridge, 60 m east of the Mathematical Bridge (1749).

- The Region R4 will have the first capitals in

New Delhi (India) and Novosibirsk (Russia) – assistance from Magdeburg (Germany).

- The Region R5 will have the first capitals in

Krasnoyarsk (Russia) and Urumqi (China) – assistance from Avignon (France).

- The Region R6 will have the first capitals in

Jakarta (Indonesia) and Beijing (China) – assistance from Neuchâtel (Switzerland).

- The Region R7 will have the first capitals in

Tokyo (Japan) and Sydney (Australia) – assistance from Malmö (Sweden).

- The Region R8 will have the first capitals in

Washington (USA) and Mexico City (Mexico) – assistance from Bellinzona (Switzerland).

- The Region R9 will have the first capitals in

Halifax (Canada) and Brasilia (Brazil) – assistance from Biel (Switzerland).

Mount Fuji (3,776 m, 1707 last eruption) seen from Kawaguchi city (down), near Kawaguchiko (Lake Kawaguchi, 6 km², 830 m elevation, has an island), 100 km south-west of Tokyo.

Mount Fuji (Fuji-san) is Japan's highest and most important mountain, from physical, cultural and spiritual point of view. The almost perfectly symmetrical cone of Mount Fuji is a symbol of Japan, and a frequent subject of Japanese art. The Japanese artist Katsushika Hokusai (1760 – 1849), born in Edo (now Tokyo) is the author of the woodblock print series 'Thirty six Views of Mount Fuji' (circa 1831) and 'One Hundred Views of Mount Fuji'.

Mount Fuji has appeared in the Japanese literature for many centuries. The summit has been considered to be a sacred place since ancient times. Mount Fuji is located on the main island Honshu, and is visible from Tokyo on a clear day, being covered by snow for half of the year. Because of its high altitude, the weather around Mount Fuji changes very quickly, and clouds are often moving across the peak, obscuring the view from time to time.

The best views of Mount Fuji are from the Fuji-Hakone-Izu National Park, near one of the five lakes that surround Mount Fuji: Kawaguchiko (Lake Kawaguchi), Lake Motosu (140 m deep), Saiko (Lake Sai, known as the Western Lake), Shojiko (Lake Shoji is the smallest), and Lake Yamanaka (the largest and easternmost, is also the third highest lake in Japan, at 980 m elevation).

Question 13. When did the alphabet writing started?

Response 13: Around 1800 BC the alphabetic writing started. Also, from this time period there are:
- from Egypt, the Moscow Mathematical Papyrus has findings of the volume of a frustum;
- from Egypt, 19th dynasty, circa 1200 BC, the Berlin Papyrus 6619 contains a quadratic equation and its solution.

This shows advanced thinking, which could have helped to better manage the world, but the wars destroyed very much.

The harmony is a precious human value, reflecting compatibility and accord in many areas, like feelings, actions, relationships, opinions and interests – exactly what is needed for a good advanced civilization.

Level 4 very friendly 10 Advisers of the world, who will supervise and assist the 10 L3 managers of the 10 regions of the Earth, for a total of about 7,700,000,000 people – all the people on Earth, citizens of Peaceful Terra.

Question 14. When the first Olympic Games were organized?

Response 14: - On 1 July 776 BC the Greeks organized the first recorded Ancient Olympic Games, with the help of people having mathematical skills.

Just imagine having 2,797 Olympic Games, one per year, instead of the tens of thousands of wars and conflicts – how much better off would we all be today!

Harmony means a state of balance among different ideas, with the purpose of advancing and getting better.

The L4 very friendly 10 Advisers of the world will be located each in one the ten Regions R0, R1,..., R9. For example, in the beginning, for the first month (then changing every month), the ten Advisers of the world will be located:

- in R0: Barcelona (Spain)
- in R1: Benghazi (Libya)
- in R2: Addis Ababa (Ethiopia)
- in R3: Hyderabad (Pakistan)
- in R4: Bhopal (India)
- in R5: Mandalay (Myanmar)
- in R6: Nanchong (China)
- in R7: Khabarovsk (Russia)
- in R8: Houston (USA)
- in R9: Recife (Brazil)

These ten L4 Advisers will be in permanent contact with each other, and with the L3 Advisers, for the best management of the world.

The ten L4 Advisers will move each month from a first capital of a region to the second capital of another region, at random (or based on urgency, if an emergency occurred). This mobility is essential for having a long period of tranquility and harmony.

The Advisors will be located in the current government buildings, and the excess government buildings and properties will be sold, in order to increase the budget, and to reduce the expenses.

The top 10 Advisers (and all the others) will collaborate via e-mail, telephone, videoconferences, mail, or face to face, when needed, to produce practical results for all people, very fast.

France, Paris: Place de la Concorde (Louis XV, 1772, 359 m by 212 m, 8.64 ha), with sumptuous light poles.

Question 15. What Thales of Miletus did for all of us?

Response 15: The first great mathematician, astronomer and philosopher - **Thales of Miletus** (c. 624 BC – 547 BC, aged 77), 54 years older than Pythagoras; when Thales died Pythagoras was 23. Thales' theorem states that if A, B and C are points on a circle, where the line AC is a diameter of the circle, then the angle ABC is a right angle. On 28 May 585 BC, Thales, 39, predicted a solar eclipse. He also said that water is the basic element of nature. Also from Miletus was **Anaximenes of Miletus** (585 BC - 528 BC, aged 57, 15 years older than Pythagoras (Anaximenes died when Pythagoras was 42)). He was a Greek philosopher and mathematician.

Harmony is a sine qua non requirement for good management, because all the decisions will be by consensus only.

It is expected that the 10 Advisors are talented enough to be able to negotiate fast any disagreements between them, and quickly arrive at the best common decision, for the benefit of all people.

Question 16. What are the contributions of Pythagoras to our civilization?

Response 16: **Pythagoras** (570 BC – 495 BC, aged 75) was a very great Greek mathematician and philosopher. Pythagoras of Samos was born on the Samos Island, which is a Greek island in the eastern Aegean Sea, just 1.6 km from the coast of Asia Minor, where is Turkey, about 250 km east of Athens, and 350 km north-east of Crete. Pythagoras married Theano, and they had four children: Damo, Myia, Telauges and Arignote. Pythagoras' mother was Pythais, and father Mnesarchus, a merchant who came from Tyre. Pythagoras died in Metapontum, which was an important ancient Greek city of Magna Graecia, currently in the Southern Italy, on the gulf of Tarentum, about 140 km east of Napoli (Naples), and 160 km northeast of Messina, Sicilia (Sicily).

Pythagoras' theorem: In any right triangle, the area of the square on the hypotenuse (opposite the right angle) is equal to the sum of the areas of the squares on the other two sides of the triangle.

Pythagoras' quotes: "Were it not for number and its nature, nothing that exists would be clear to anybody, either in itself, or in its relation to other things...You can observe the power of number exercising itself ... in all acts and the thoughts of men, in all handicrafts and music." "As soon as laws are necessary for men, they are no longer fit for freedom."

About 530 BC, Pythagoras, 40, discovered the dependence of musical intervals on the arithmetical ratios of the lengths of string at the same tension, 2:1 giving an octave. He also discovered a general formula for finding two square numbers the sum of which is also a square. The Pythagoreans and Plato noted that the conclusions they reached deductively agreed to a remarkable extent with the results of observation and inductive inference, therefore mathematics is the study of ultimate, eternal reality, immanent in nature and the universe. The Pythagoreans developed the theory of geometric magnitudes, by which they were able to compare two surfaces' ratio. He also discovered the irrationality of the square root of two.

Living in peace and harmony with ourselves an all the people around means living and working together peacefully, for the benefit of all.

The ten L4 Advisers will be elected from the 10 regions, and each of them will be the First Adviser (*First among equals* – from Latin: Primus inter pares) for one month, by rotation.

The First Adviser only coordinates the work of the other 9 Advisors for one month.

USA, Chicago (1833): Chicago Water Works (down, 1869, was pumping station, survived fire in 1871, now base for the Lookingglass Theatre Company), Water Tower Place (right, 1976, 74 fl, 261 m), John Hancock Center (left up, 1969, 100 fl, 457 m with antenna).

Question 17. Is Confucius important today?

Response 17: Very much indeed - **Confucius** is the founder of Confucianism, and the Confucius Temple in Qufu was built to honor him — the great philosopher and educator who lived from 551 BC to 479 BC (aged 72, he was 19 years younger than Pythagoras, and when Pythagoras died, Confucius was 56).

To maintain a peaceful and harmonious atmosphere for all people, the 10 Advisers will be using a Monthly World Report.

The First Adviser, on the last day of each month, will present in writing for the world (no more than 5 standard pages) a clear and precise Monthly World Report, with a list of finished and unfinished tasks.

The other 9 Advisers will add their comments to the Monthly World Report (no more than half a page each - total report less than 9.5 pages).

In order to better know the world government, to help it, and, especially, to improve it, all able people of the world will work as volunteers at least one day per year in each of the seven departments.

After each Monthly World Report, a public opinion survey about the report should be taken, and presented to all Advisors.

All activities of the Advisors, and others from the small World Government, will be available to the people on a website.

Girl with Sheaf of Corn by Auguste Renoir, 35, 1876, (25 February 1841 – 3 December 1919, aged 78.8, French painter).

Question 18. When the democracy was created?

Response 18: Democracy was instituted at Athens, Greece, in 508 BC, when Pythagoras was 62, and Confucius 43.

Now, just for a moment, imagine that the world would have had over 2,529 years of democracy, and the followers of Pythagoras, and Confucius would have continued to advance our civilization, without any wars – we would be at least 500 years more advanced than we are today!

Harmony has a high priority for all Advisers.

The top 10 Advisers will manage Police and all other Departments.

For obvious uncooperative or improper attitude of one top Advisor X, the other 9 can replace X with X's number 2, and X will receive appropriate medical treatment.

When vacancies happen for Advisors, the number 2 for those Advisors will fill the vacancies.

All the activities of all Advisors will be recorded in computers and videos, and on paper, for people to be able to see what they are doing.

Advisors at all levels should work 40 hours/week, with 4 weeks of vacation, but many services (medical, police (firemen should be part of the police), emergency, volunteers) should be non-stop.

Advisors' compensation should be the world annual average salary (in 2019 less than $10,000) plus 4% of that world average salary, for level 4 (total $10,400), + 3 % for level 3, and so on. They all should work to increase the world average salary, in order to get themselves an increase.

All the other world government employees will have a compensation close to the average compensation of the people in the area where they are located.

All Advisors are free to speak about their administrative work, with modesty.

At least 7 of the top 10 Advisers should be present every working day.

Japan, Inzai: Wind turbine working on the north-west part of the Inzai (Chiba) campus of Tokyo Denki University, 34 km north-east of Tokyo.

Question 19. When the Classical Sanskrit and zero appeared?

Response 19: Around 500 BC (Pythagoras was 70, and Confucius 51) - **Panini** standardizes the grammar and morphology of Sanskrit, in the text Ashtadhyayi, which is known as Classical Sanskrit.

Pingala uses zero and the binary numeral system.

Nobody needs war!

Advisors (and all the others) cannot declare war, reprisals or capture land or water.

Advisors (and all the others) cannot raise and support armies, navy, or any military forces.

Niagara Falls (8000 BC, the highest flow rate in the world), with the American Falls (left, USA, 21-30 m drop, 290 m wide), the Bridal Veil Falls (center-left, USA, 21 m drop, 10 m wide) and the Horseshoe Falls (center, in Canada, 53 m drop, 790 m wide).

Question 20. Who first formulated the atomic theory of the universe?

Response 20: **<u>Democritus</u>** (c. 460 BC – c. 370 BC, aged c. 90; he was 10 years younger than Socrates (470 BC – 399 BC, aged 71), same age as Hippocrates (460 BC – 375 BC), and was born 19 years after Confucius died). He was a Greek philosopher, mathematician and astronomer, who formulated an atomic theory of the universe, becoming a father of modern science. He announced, when he was 75, in 385 BC (when Plato was 43), that the Milky Way (Via Lactea, which includes the Solar System, and this Solar System is about 27,000 light-years from the Milky Way (or Galactic) Center) is a concentration of many distant stars (200 - 400 billions).

Because of too many wars, the discoveries of Democritus were temporarily or permanently lost, and the advancement of civilization was postponed.

Each Advisor, and each manager at all levels, will have 5 immediate assistants:
1) a mathematician for finance and all other calculations,
2) a medical doctor for keeping everybody healthy, calm, polite, friendly and optimist,
3) a CEO for good management,
4) an engineer for all practical projects, and
5) a teacher for education, training and related areas.

The five assistants play a key role, because they are highly qualified professionals, who actually will carry on the practical management of the world.

The five assistants' integrity, professionalism and friendliness will significantly improve the quality of the world and local governments.

The five assistants are really the experts. They will assist the Advisors and all levels of management, in order to have an efficient, correct and professional working of the world government at all levels.

All spending proposals from Advisers must be approved by their 5 assistants (doctors, mathematicians, CEOs, engineers and teachers), and must have an already existing funding in the budget.

Paris - The central part of the façade of L'Opéra de Paris (1875): composers Daniel Auber (1782–1871, left), Ludwig van Beethoven (1770–1827, second), Wolfgang Amadeus Mozart (1756–1791, center) and Gaspare Spontini (1774–1851, right).

Japan, Tokyo: In Shinjuku, from the 45th fl., 202 m, of Tokyo Met. Gov Bldg.): Shinjuku Mitsui Building (224 m, 55 floors, 1974, left), Shinjuku Center Building (223 m, 54 floors, 1979, center), Mode Gakuen Cocoon Tower (204 m, 50 floors, 2008, right up), Keio Plaza Hotel (180 m, 47 fl, 1971, right).

Question 21. What is the importance of Hippocrates?

Response 21: **Hippocrates** (c. 460 BC, Island of Cos, Greece — c. 375 BC, Larissa, Thessaly, Greece, aged 85, same age as Democritus, but died 5 years before him), Greek philosopher and physician, who wrote the Corpus Hippocraticum - he is the father of medicine. He began the scientific study of medicine, and prescribed a form of aspirin. Hippocrates' quotes:

"Wherever the art of medicine is loved, there is also a love of humanity."

"Make a habit of two things: to help; or at least to do no harm."

Hippocrates is essential today, because his recommendations are the medical foundation of the coming new global structure.

Understanding other people is a generator of harmony and peace.

An Honorific World Observer will be quietly elected by direct vote – starting, for example, 1st September 2022 - for only one 3 years term, with the main duty to observe that the top 10 Advisers efficiently perform their duties, and keep their words – if they don't, they will be changed.

For managers and for everybody else, keeping their word is a serious and strict requirement.

The Honorific World Observer has this responsibility for the top 10 Advisors, but all people will pay attention to this. Words must become again important and respected.

Question 22. Who created mathematical mechanics, and was a good friend of Plato?

Response 22: **Archytas** (c. 428 BC – 347 BC, aged c. 81, 32 years younger than Hippocrates). He was an Ancient Greek philosopher, mathematician, astronomer, statesman, and strategist. He was a scientist of the Pythagorean school (create 70 years before Archytas' birth), and famous for being the reputed founder of mathematical mechanics, as well as a good friend of Plato, who was one year younger than Archytas, and they died in the same year. He created the Archytas curve, solved the Delian Problem (doubling the cube), worked on the harmonic theory of music, which was adopted and adapted by Plato and later Aristotle, and he explains that the space is infinite, which is true.

Clarity and harmony are the foundation of the World Government, because the communication with people is based on this foundation.

All the employees of the World Government are temporary, and must reapply for their positions every year.

There is no need for unions.

The World Government will be limited to:
1) the Office of the Honorific Observer (less than 10 employees),
2) the Office of the top ten Advisors (less than 100 employees), and
3) 7 small departments.

Question 23. What is the importance of Plato?

Response 23: **Plato** (7 May 427 BC – 347 BC, aged 80), great Greek philosopher, student of Socrates (43 years older than Plato), one year younger than Archytas, teacher of Aristotle (43 years younger than Plato), the founder of the Academy in Athens, the first institution of higher learning in the world. Plato's quotes:

"Access to power must be confined to those who are not in love with it."

"Any man may easily do harm, but not every man can do good to another."

"Excess generally causes reaction, and produces a change in the opposite direction, whether it be in the seasons, or in individuals, or in governments."

Obviously, these quotes, and many other of the Plato's quotes, are the foundation of a good society, which will soon be implemented.

The World Government will have these 7 small departments:

- Tax Department

- Collects taxes of 15% of the income of people and revenue of companies.

- The Manager of the Tax Department is appointed for a three-year term by the World 10 Advisers.

- The number of employees must be under 50,000, with excellent computers, and advanced software.

USA, Niagara Falls (8000 BC, the highest flow rate in the world), with the American Falls (left, USA, 21-30 m drop, 290 m wide), the Bridal Veil Falls (center, USA, 21 m drop, 10 m wide) and the Horseshoe Falls (center-right, in Canada, 53 m drop, 790 m wide).

- Treasury

Treasury will control all the financial issues, including:
- antitrust
- fiscal service
- financial cooperation
- financing bank
- world reserve system
- world budget using only revenue, no borrowing, and spending only on strict necessary needs
– all the budgets, at all levels, will have a 2% surplus, which will be returned to the taxpayers
- register of all government papers and activities
- archives and records
- assist all people to have savings accounts for old age (the old age will be starting around 70), and 10% of their income should automatically go to their savings accounts. For those unable to work, their doctors and mathematicians will decide case by case.
- bankruptcies, in general, will be discouraged, and when strict necessary, will be analyzed and solved, case by case, by the doctors, mathematicians and CEOs who worked with the people who asked the bankruptcy.
- encourage all families to assist their parents, grandparents, and great-grandparents.
- housing finance
- housing for all people
- no homelessness
- consumer financial protection
- pensions
- privacy
- current social security until replaced by personal savings
- personnel management
- general services for the world government
- each the 10 regions will receive 2.5% of the world taxes - at least 30% of the money will be sent to villages and cities.
- each of the 100 sub-regions will receive 0.25% of the world taxes. At least 40% of the money will be sent to villages and cities.

- The World Central Bank will include all current central banks – starting, for example, on May 1st, 2023.
- The Special Credit Card (SCC) will be issued by the World Central Bank.
- Advisors will create a new world currency, named, for example, "coin", and all the other currencies will be exchanged for coins. The World Central Bank will implement the details.
- The counterfeiting and all other bad things, which some sick people do, will be medically treated (in specialized medical institutions when necessary), and those who did bad things will pay all the expenses, and will reimburse the victims. Victims will always be very protected, and helped to recover the losses from the attackers.

Japan, Osaka (645 AD, the 3rd largest city in Japan, capital of Osaka Prefecture on the main island Honshu): detail of Toyosaki shrine (1772, with the Emperor Kotoku and others enshrined here).

- People Assistance Department

It will assist people in general, including:
- parent assistance
- dispute resolution
- in very simple disputes or culpa levis (ordinary negligence, like late payments, etc.), one single assistant will decide within minutes, and all people will go back to work
- census every 5 years
- election assistance every 20 months
 - special credit cards
- people protection against abuses from anybody
- completely eliminate corruption, organized crime and drug trafficking
- all people in the world will remain in their places, and the improvements will come to them. Those who want to move to other places, will need first a special invitation from at least 10 people (not family related) where they want to move.
- all the Tribunals and related areas will be transformed in people assistance services, based on friendliness, collaboration and goodwill.
- It is well understood that no excessive bail will be required, no excessive fines imposed, no cruel and unusual punishments applied, but, at the same time, it is well understood that a person who did a bad thing will receive the necessary corrective medical treatment, and will reimburse all people who suffered damages, and the medical treatment. The victims will always receive special attention.
- Nobility (King, Prince, etc.) could continue to exist in some places, but they should not interfere with activities of the Advisors, and actually should help them.
- food safety
- trash & recycling
- free commerce
- jobs assistance
- postal service
- labor safety and harmonious relations
- land, water

- volunteers
- because late payments are very frequent sources of conflict, the world government will have sufficient people to solve these small issues promptly, for a small fee (like 1% of the amount).
- fitness, sport, tourism
- 10 world holidays: the normal 4 Earth events (2 solstices (around 21 June, around 21 December), and 2 equinoxes (around 21 March, around 21 September), Mother's Day on 1st May, Father's Day on 6 August, Children's Day on 6 November, Grandparents' Day on 6 February, and 2 optional days (like Thanksgiving or a Religious Day (Christmas), and New Year).

Japan, Inzai Post Office, 300 m north-est from the main entrance to the Inzai (Chiba) campus of Tokyo Denki University (TDU, founded in 1907) in Muzai-Gakuendai, 34 km north-east of Tokyo.

- Medical Department

It will manage all medical and healthcare related areas, including:
- human services
- conflict resolution
- families, children, elderly
- medicine approval
- disease control and prevention
- medical doctors and assistants will make regular home visits, at least once a year, to all people, to keep them healthy, and to prevent illnesses.
- medical research: cancer, heart, lung, blood, arthritis, surgical robotics, connected computers for healthcare, etc.
- healthy homes, streets, stores, working places, etc.
- healthy aging
- all misunderstandings, disagreements or conflicts of any nature will be treated by medical personnel (with police help when strict necessary), until all is back to normal.
- no prisons are necessary, only specialized medical institutions (in simple cases, the places where the treated people live can be used, with the necessary limitations and surveillance)
- If a person X is considered that did a bad thing, X will have, within 3 days, a discussion with one or more doctors and other assistants, and will be informed of the nature and cause of the bad thing; including witnesses against and for him. Then a decision will be taken within other 3 days, by a group of doctors and other assistants. Victims of bad people will always have priority to discuss their problems with one or more doctors and other assistants, and quick decisions will be taken within 3 days, by a group of doctors and other assistants. Protection of victims has always priority.
- in order to better know the world government, to help it, and, especially, to improve it, all able people of the world will work as volunteers at least one day per year in the local facility of this department, which will have a special office for managing this volunteer work.

 – all people will have government medical insurance, and they can also have private medical insurance
 – there will be doctors working for the government 100%, or only part-time, or having only private practice, all with reasonable salaries and fees.
 – there will be government pharmaceutical institutions and private pharmaceutical companies, offering reasonable priced medicines, without advertising to the general public.

USA, Washington (1790), National Gallery of Art (1937, National Mall).

- Police

Police will provide assistance for:
- accidents
- disasters
- complete elimination of nuclear, chemical and biological arms, firearms and explosives
- world complete security
- world cooperation
- conflict reduction and resolution
- investigations
- emergency assistance
- training
- delinquency prevention in general, and especially juvenile
- protection of Advisors, important government buildings, etc.
- extended surveillance and reconnaissance to prevent bad events
- fire protection
- volunteers to help police
- police will be present at public meetings, services, shows, etc., in order to protect the public
- public order
- ensuring traffic safety
- completely eliminate corruption, organized crime and drug trafficking
- movement of people based on civilized rules
- assist and protect those who have encountered violence
- World Police and specialists from the former United Nations and Interpol will be ready and very mobile for urgent and special operations, when they are needed.
- Police will be the only department which will have some small arms, in order to stop some very bad people (who are very sick).
- a small manufacturing and maintenance of arms unit will be part of the Police Department, under strict control.
- Police will work with medical personnel, mathematicians, CEOs, engineers, teachers and others, to make sure that all the people on the Planet are in good mental health, in order to prevent bad situations. This is also a major responsibility of all Advisors.

- prevention of bad events
- The Advisors will allocate the necessary budget for Police, and Police will assist people in need.

Japan, 13 km north-east from Mount Fuji, the easternmost and largest of the five lakes, Lake Yamanaka is also the third highest lake in Japan, standing at 980 meters above sea level.

- Education Department

- Over 2 billions of children in the world will get a solid peace-oriented education, to give a solid peace-oriented foundation for a good, free, peaceful and prosperous life.
- Education is very important – teachers will work with parents and grandparents, to educate the children to leave healthy in a sustainable peace, liberty and prosperity.
- Discipline must be strict, and those who do not behave properly, will get medical assistance.
- The world will have 4 school levels (SLs) of education:
SL1 – Kindergarten – 2 years: age 5 and 6
SL2 – Primary School – 4 years: age 7, 8, 9 and 10
SL3 – Secondary School – 3 years: age 11, 12 and 13
SL4 – High School or Vocational School – 4 years: age 14, 15, 16 and 17
- A World Library will include the Library of Congress and all the other great libraries – they will remain where they are now, but will be digitally interconnected, and accessible from any place in the world.
- adult education: technical, career
- training for employment
- management training
- post high school education
- peace education
- world constitution education

Italy, Rome (753 BC, one of the oldest cities in Europe, called Roma Aeterna (The Eternal City) and Caput Mundi (Capital of the World)), from the Pincian Hill looking southwest: Piazza del Popolo (1822), with the Egyptian obelisk (36 m) of Sety I (1290–1279 BC) and Rameses II (1303, 1279–1213 BC) from Heliopolis, brought in 10 BC by Augustus (63 BC-14 AD) for Circus Maximus, in 1589 here. Basilica San Pietro (1506, 132 m, back).

- Science & Technology Department.

It will help in the areas of:
- mathematics
- statistics
- science
- technology
- Algorithmic Governance will be an essential tool for a better and impartial governing of the world, used by the Advisers elected by people. Mathematicians from all countries will work to improve the Algorithmic Governance, to better serve the people.
- cyberspace complete security will be achieved and strictly maintained
- information systems
- computer services
- Internet
- scientific cooperation
- economic development at the world level
- infrastructure improvement and maintenance at the world level
- innovation and improvements in all areas, at the world level
- transportation at the world level
- safety
- security
- aviation
- highway
- cars
- railroads without noise
- maritime administration
- logistics
- strategic planning at the world level
- public works
- fleet maintenance
- standards: weights, measures, etc.
- research at the world level
- risk analysis
- laboratories
- engineering

- communications at the world level
- telecommunications
- networks
- peaceful nuclear energy use at the world level
- safety
- waste
- electrical power
- oceanic analysis at the world level
- atmospheric analysis at the global level
- meteorological service and prognosis at the global level
- world resources analysis
- sustainable use of world resources
- geographical and geological activity
- product safety at the global level
- hazardous material and chemical safety
- government broadcasting (radio, tv, Internet, newspaper, etc.) including news, scientific and technical information
- private broadcasting will continue, but the world government must be able to directly inform the people, without intermediaries
- space exploration and expansion at the world level – very important for the future
- patent and trademark
- intellectual rights
- all government work, which can be done by private companies, will be contracted with the best and reasonably priced private companies. At the same time, the government should always have competitive services for people – from plumbing and electrical help, to mortgage and buying or selling a house.

Italy, Rome: The east side of the Mausoleum (135-139) of Hadrian (76–138, Emperor 117-138, renamed Castel Sant'Angelo in 600). It was used by the popes as a castle and now is a museum.

Question 24. Who proved that there are precisely five regular convex polyhedra?

Response 24: **Theaetetus of Athens** (c. 417, Athens – c. 369 BC, aged c. 48). He was a Greek mathematician, who had contributions on irrational lengths, which were included in Book X of Euclid's Elements, and proving that there are precisely five regular convex polyhedra. A younger friend of Socrates (53 years older than him – when Socrates died, he was 18), and Plato (who was 10 years older than him – when Theaetetus died, Plato was 58), he is the central character in Plato's eponymous Socratic dialogue. Theaetetus, like Plato, was a student of the Greek mathematician Theodorus of Cyrene. Cyrene was a prosperous Greek colony (founded in 631 BC, and abandoned after about 1,000 years, around 370) on the coast of North Africa, in what is now Libya, on the eastern end of the Gulf of Sidra, 600 km southwest of Athens, and 780 km northwest of Alexandria in Egypt. Theodorus had explored the theory of incommensurable quantities, and Theaetetus continued those studies - he classified various forms of irrational numbers according to the way they are expressed as square roots. This theory is presented in great detail in Book X of Euclid's Elements. Most of what we know of him comes from Plato, who named a dialogue after him, the Theaetetus. The crater Theaetetus on the Moon is named after him.

The Advisers should be elected every 20 months for one term only. If an Adviser X was elected for a term T1, then the next term T2 will have another Advisor Y. For the next term T3, X can be elected again, but the next term T4 will have a new Adviser, and so on. All levels of Advisers (minimum age 25 years) can be elected, not consecutively, at most 4 times (maximum 80 months = 6 years and 8 months).

All the employees in Government will respect Seneca's (circa 1,960 years ago) aphorism "To govern is to serve, not to rule", and Hippocrates' (over 2,400 years ago) aphorism "Make a habit of two things: to help; or at least to do no harm."

Advisers should have exceptional results obtained from their work, and based on these results, plus modesty, moderation, good character, friendliness, sharp mind, wisdom, good morals, and intense desire to help people, they will be elected, without any campaigning, publicity, fundraising, donations, debates, propaganda, political parties, advertising, or similar activities.

There will be use of advanced digital technology, which opens up entirely new opportunities for developing direct elections, and public control of the institutions, improving the transparency of the election procedure, and taking into account the interests and opinions of each voter (over the age of 21, who are not in a special medical institution for bad behavior or for mental health).

USA, New York: On W 42nd St, the northeast façade of the New York Public Library (1902).

Question 25. Who attempted to find the total number of syllables that could be made from the letters of the alphabet?

Response 25: **<u>Xenocrates</u>** (c. 395 BC – 313 BC, aged c. 82, 22 years younger than Theaetetus of Athens) of Chalcedon (an ancient maritime town of Bithynia, in Asia Minor, located almost directly opposite to Byzantium, south of Scutari, and now a district of the city of Istanbul named Kadıköy. The name Chalcedon is a variant of Calchedon, found on all the coins of the town, as well as in manuscripts of Herodotus's Histories, Xenophon's Hellenica, Arrian's Anabasis, and other works). He was a Greek philosopher, mathematician, and leader (scholarch) of the Platonic Academy for 26 years, from 339 BC (age 56) to 313 BC (age 82). His teachings followed those of Plato, which he attempted to define more closely, often with mathematical elements. Xenocrates wrote a book On Numbers, and a Theory of Numbers, besides books on geometry. Plutarch writes that Xenocrates once attempted to find the total number of syllables that could be made from the letters of the alphabet. According to Plutarch, Xenocrates result was 1,002,000,000,000 (1 trillion and 2 billions). This possibly represents the first instance that a combinatorial problem involving permutations was attempted.

An Election Commission of 110 representatives from the 10 regions and from the 100 sub-regions, elected separately for 5 years, will have to examine the qualifications of all the candidates for Advisers, and for other senior management positions. Unqualified candidates will be asked to improve their qualifications, and then to try again later.

It is important to refresh the management, and to bring new people to help the big family of 7.7 B people. The older generations, who performed well, will be retained in important roles, because experience and maturity count very much. At least two months before the retirement, they will kindly be asked to transfer their expertise to the younger generation. Even after retirement, they will occasionally be invited to share their expertise.

In every election, with every winner, will be other two for number 2 and number 3. The number 2 and number 3 for each management position will be used when number 1 is not available (vacation, sick, etc.). They will constantly work for number 1, helping to solve urgent problems for the people.

Good elections are essential for the future.

There has been a tendency to make elections conflict generating events, with lots of propaganda, false information, heavy donations, unpolite confrontations, bully fundraising, hostile political parties and organizations, unlimited power ambitions, etc.

This will be completely changed into clean, friendly elections, in which people choose between leaders with outstanding results, plus talent to lead people to peace and freedom, modesty, moderation, good character, friendliness, sharp mind, wisdom, good morals, and intense desire to help people – no campaigning, no publicity, no fundraising, no donations, no debates, no propaganda, no political parties, no advertising, or similar activities.

All Advisors should also be local Administrators – they must show that they are good managers, and produce practical results for all people.

Italy, Venezia, Palazzo Dandolo on Riva degli Schiavoni, 150 m east of Piazza San Marco.

Question 26. Who first stated that the Earth rotates on its axis, from west to east, once every 24 hours?

Response: **Heraclides Ponticus** (c. 390 BC – c. 310 BC, aged c. 80, 5 years younger than Xenocrates). He was a Greek philosopher and astronomer who was born in Heraclea Pontica (on the southwest of the Black Sea, 760 km northeast of Athens, 400 km southeast of Tomis (now Constanta, Romania), now Karadeniz Ereğli, Turkey), and migrated to Athens. He correctly stated that the Earth rotates on its axis, from west to east, once every 24 hours.

An electronic world referendum will be organized every three months. The main questions will be:

1. Are you satisfied with the Government?
2. What Government work is good?
3. What Government work is not good?
4: Suggestions for improvement:

Within two months after each referendum, the Government will respond to the people. Based on the suggestions received, new pro-people rules will be replacing some old rules.

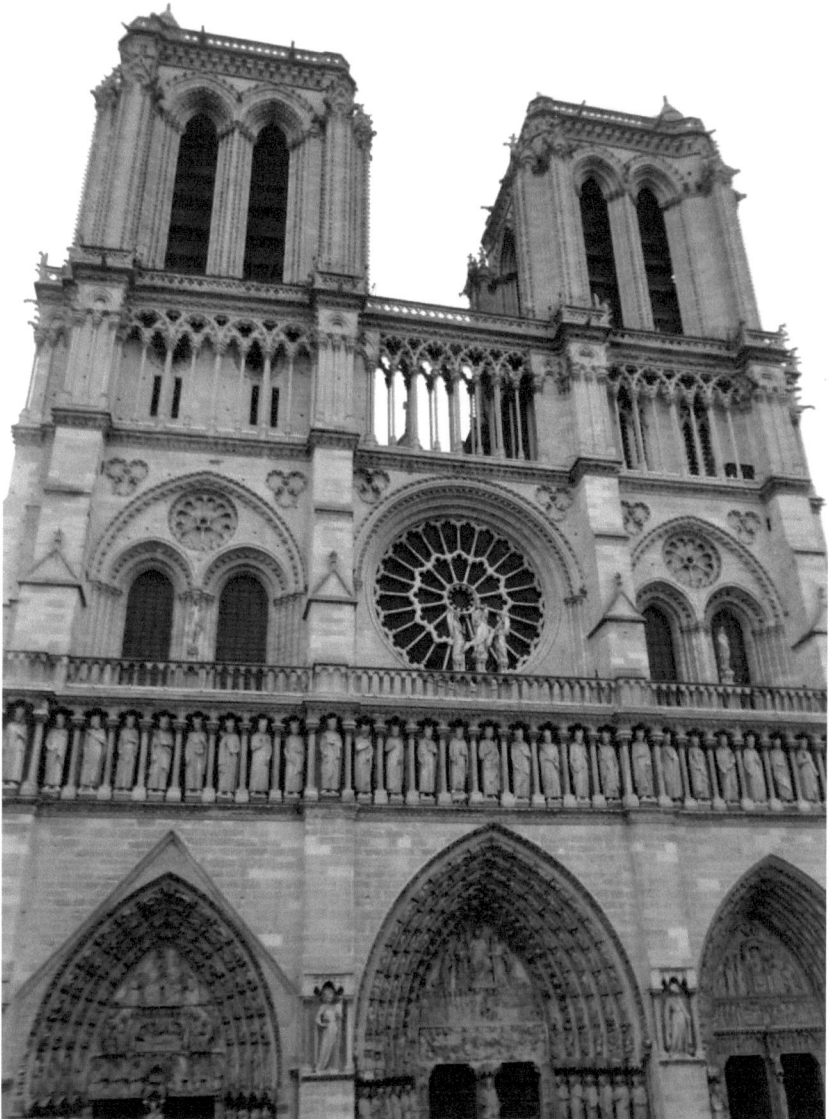

France: The upper part of the western façade of Cathédrale Notre Dame de Paris (1163 – 1345, 90 m), on the south-eastern part of the Île de la Cité, which is considered the center of Paris, in the fourth arrondissement. The organ has 7,374 pipes, with about 900 classified as historical. It has 110 real stops, five 56-key manuals and a 32-key pedalboard; it is now fully computerized. The Towers at Notre-Dame contain five church bells. The great bourdon bell, Emmanuel, from 1681, 13 t, is located in the South Tower (right).

Question 27. What is the importance of Aristotle?

Response: **<u>Aristotle</u>** (384 BC – 2 Oct 322 BC, aged 62). He was a great Greek philosopher and scientist, student of Plato (43 years older than Aristotle), and teacher of Alexander the Great (20 July 356 BC – 10 June 323 BC, aged 32 years 10 months and 21 days, 28 years younger than Aristotle). In 350 BC, Aristotle, 34, discusses logical reasoning in Organon.

With his logical reasoning, Aristotle is very important today.

Arms will not exist anymore, and only the police will have some small arms. Those who want arms for hunting or sport, will borrow them from police stations, with proper documents, rules and payments.

All military units will become strong civilian organizations, working to improve the quality of life for everybody.

For practical reasons, the transition from the current imperfect situation to the much better Sustainable Peace and Prosperity Structure (SPPS) will be very smooth: first - all the countries remain as they are, and they will begin – for example on January 1st, 2022 - to negotiate total and complete disarmament, with the help of the United Nations, for 3 months. Then for 5 months will intensely work to eliminate all the arms – either transform them in peaceful tools, or destroy them. Then a continuous verification and monitoring will be implemented, the make sure that the world finally achieved complete disarmament forever!

Question 28. Who discovered the conic sections?

Response: **Menaechmus** (380 BC – 320 BC, aged 60, 4 years younger than Aristotle). He was an ancient Greek mathematician born in a city on the Thracian Chersonese (now Gallipoli peninsula, with the Aegean Sea to the west and the Dardanelles strait to the east), who was a 47 years younger friend of Plato. Menaechmus is known for his discovery of conic sections, and for his solution to the problem of doubling the cube using the parabola and hyperbola.

A census will take place every 5 years – starting, for example, on October 1st, 2023 - and all people will receive a special credit card (SCC), with their photo and other personal data. The delimitations between regions, and between sub-regions, will be adjusted by the census.

Italy, Cividale del Friuli: 3 Nov 2009, on Corso Paolino d'Aquileia, on the bridge of Iacopo da Bissone (1442, 50 m by 3.6 m, height 22.5 m, rock) over Natisone River (flowing from back to front), 150 m southeast of Palazzo Comunale, looking northeast to il Campanile of Monastero Santa Maria in Valle (650, up left) and Natisone River.

Japan, Tokyo: In Shinjuku, from the 45th fl., 202 m, of Tokyo Met. Gov Bldg. South Tower): part of the North Tower of Tokyo Met. Gov Bldg. (243 m, 48 fl, 1991, left), Shinjuku Sumitomo Bldg. (210 m, 52 fl, 1974, center), Shinjuku Mitsui Building (224 m, 55 floors, 1974, right),

Question 29. Who was the first historian of science?

Response: **<u>Eudemus of Rhodes</u>** (c. 370 BC - c. 300 BC, aged c. 70, 10 years younger than Menaechmus). He was an ancient Greek philosopher, considered the first historian of science. He was one of Aristotle's most important pupils, 14 years younger than Aristotle, editing his teacher's work, and making it more easily accessible. Eudemus' nephew, Pasicles, was also credited with editing Aristotle's works.

Without wars, the history would be much better and nicer.

The special credit card (SCC) will be used to buy everything, to identify for voting, for census, for travel, for medical assistance, etc.

The current private credit cards will continue to work as usual.

The changes of the delimitations between regions, and also sub-regions, will be inputted on these cards, and no other work is needed.

Question 30. Why is Euclid so important?

Response: **Euclid** (325 BC – 265 BC, aged 60, 45 years younger than Eudemus, and 59 years younger than Aristotle, who died 3 years after the birth of Euclid). He was a great Greek mathematician, and the father of geometry. He arrived with his parents in Alexandria in 322 BC, when he was 3 years old, about ten years after Alexandria's founding, in 332 BC, by Alexander the Great, 24, (356 BC – 323 BC, aged 32.9). It is probable that he attended Plato's Academy in Athens, and received his mathematical training from students of Plato (who died 22 years before the birth of Euclid). He was active in Alexandria during the reign of Ptolemy I (323 BC – 283 BC, 40 years). Alexandria was then the largest city in the western world, and the center of both the papyrus industry, and the book trade. Ptolemy had created the great library at Alexandria, which was known as the Museum, because it was considered a house of the muses for the arts and sciences. Many scholars worked and taught there, and this is the place where Euclid wrote The Elements. His 13 books Elements, based on the works of Thales, Pythagoras, Plato, Eudoxus, Aristotle, Menaechmus and others, are the most influential books in the history of mathematics, the most famous, and most published mathematical work in history, serving as the main textbook for teaching mathematics (especially geometry) from the time of its publication (around 280 BC, when Euclid was 45 years old) for more than 2200 years. In the Elements, Euclid deduced the principles of what is now called Euclidean geometry, from a small set of axioms. He began with accepted mathematical truths, axioms and postulates, and demonstrated logically 467 propositions in plane and solid geometry. One of the proofs was for the theorem of Pythagoras, proving that the equation is always true for every right triangle. The books "Elements" were the most widely used textbooks of all time, have appeared in more than 1,000 editions since printing was invented, were still found in classrooms until about 50 years ago, and have sold more copies than any book other than the Bible. He introduced a system of rigorous mathematical proofs that remains the basis of mathematics to this day. Euclid also wrote works on perspective, conic sections, spherical geometry, number theory, and rigor. Euclid is the anglicized version of the Greek name, which means "renowned, glorious". Campanus translated The Elements from Arabic to Latin, and the first printed edition appeared in Venice in 1482. The first English translation of The Elements was by the mathematician John Dee in 1570. Dee's lectures and writings revived interest in mathematics in England. His translation was from a Latin translation of an Arabic translation of the original Greek. Euclid in his Elements studies geometry as an axiomatic system, proves the infinitude of prime numbers, and presents the Euclidean algorithm. He presents the law of reflection in Catoptrics, and he proves the fundamental theorem of arithmetic.

Now we can see why Euclid is so important for our civilization.

People are something sacred for people

The enemies of the people on Earth are not other people, but viruses, microbes, bad bacteria and hundreds of deadly illnesses – all people on Earth will work together, in a harmonious effort, against these real enemies for all of us.

Italy, Rome (753 BC), from cordonata capitolina (flight of steps, which can be also used by horses, with balustrades ending down with two Egyptian lions in black basalt, and up with two marble statues of Castor (left) and Pollux (right), by Michelangelo), Campidoglio (1546 by Michelangelo, on Collis Capitolinus, the oldest part of Rome, with Temple of Jupiter, 509 BC), Palazzo Senatorio (back, 1350, atop Tabularium, now the city hall).

Question 31. Who was the first to formulate the heliocentric model?

Response: **Aristarchus of Samos** (310 BC – 230 BC, aged 80, 15 years younger than Euclid). He was a Greek mathematician and astronomer, who formulated a model of the universe that placed the Sun, rather than the Earth, at the center of the universe. Because of wars and incompetence, this heliocentric model was ignored, and replaced with the geocentric model for 1,780 years, until 1543, when Nicolaus Copernicus (19 Feb 1473 – 24 May 1543, aged 70.2), independently, formulated the same heliocentric model. Aristarchus also sustained that Earth rotates on its axis, which was first observed about 50 years earlier by Heraclides Ponticus, who died when Aristarchus was born.

Very clearly, people do not want war, and people need harmonious relationships.

Non-violence is a strict requirement for all activities on Earth.

The first rule for everybody on Earth comes from the Hippocratic Oath: Primum non nocere - first do not harm, mentioned over 2,400 years ago.

Question 32. Why is Archimedes so famous?

Response: **Archimedes** (c. 287 BC Syracuse, Sicily, Magna Graecia – c. 212 BC Syracuse, Sicily, Magna Graecia, aged 75, 23 years younger than Aristarchus, and 38 years younger than Euclid). He was a Greek mathematician, physicist, engineer, inventor, and astronomer. At 17, in 270 BC, Archimedes, after discovering the water buoyancy theories, said Eureka! In 269 BC, Archimedes, 18, traveled to Alexandria to study – in the same year he re-discovered π. After 6 years, in 263 BC, Archimedes, 24, returned to Syracuse. His inventions Archimedes Claw (213 BC), screw (265 BC), and water buoyancy theories, are developed between 270 BC and 213 BC, when he was 17 to 74. Archimedes proved that the value of π lies between 3 + 1/7 (approx. 3.1429), and 3 + 10/71 (approx. 3.1408, the correct value is 3.141592…..), that the area of a circle is equal to π multiplied by the square of the radius of the circle, and that the area enclosed by a parabola and a straight line is 4/3 multiplied by the area of a triangle with equal base and height. He also gave a very accurate estimate of the value of the square root of 3. Circa 137 years after the death of Archimedes, in 75 BC, Marcus Tullius Cicero (3 Jan 106 BC – 7 Dec 43 BC, aged 63.9, Roman statesman, orator, and philosopher, who served as consul in the year 63 BC) discovered and restored Archimedes' tomb.

His discoveries and inventions make him so famous – without wars people could have used and improve his work much faster, for our benefit.

Home visits will be the real joy, and will be full of harmony.

Medical doctors and assistants will make regular home visits to all people, to keep them healthy, and to prevent illnesses.

Question 33. Who created the discipline of geography?

Response: **<u>Eratosthenes</u>** of Cyrene (Cyrene is now in Libya), (276 BC – 194 BC, aged 82, 11 years younger than Archimedes). He was a Greek mathematician, geographer, poet, astronomer, and music theorist. He was the chief librarian at the Library of Alexandria. He created the discipline of geography, including the terminology used today. On 19 June 240 BC, at age 36, he estimated the circumference of the Earth to be nearly 250,000 stadia (40,233 km (1 stadia = 0.16 km), not far from the correct equatorial circumference of 40,075 km (equatorial radius is 6,378.137 km); polar circumference is 40,007 km). Also in 240 BC, he used his sieve algorithm to quickly isolate prime numbers.

Harmony also means to have similar goals, therefore the truth is always needed!

People need only truth in order to create a long term peaceful and harmonious society.

If someone lies – medical treatment will follow.

Japan, Tokyo: In Shinjuku, from the 45th fl., 202 m, of Tokyo Metropolitan. Gov Bldg. North Tower: part of South Tower of Tokyo Metropolitan. Gov Bldg. (243 m, 48 floors, 1991, left), Shinjuku Park Tower (235 m, 52 fl, 1994, center-left), Tokyo Opera City Tower (234 m, 54 fl, 1996, center-right), Shinjuku Central Park (down).

Question 34. Who discovered that the tides are caused by the Moon?

Response: **Seleucus of Seleucia** (c. 190 BC - c. 150 BC, aged c. 40, born 4 years after the death of Eratosthenes). He was a Hellenistic astronomer and philosopher, who was a proponent of heliocentrism (like his predecessors Heraclides Ponticus, and Aristarchus), and who discovered that tides are caused by the Moon.

Freedom and harmony go hand in hand, you cannot have harmony without freedom.

Freedom is a fundamental requirement on Earth.

It is well understood that this freedom refers to doing good things in a civilized manner, not for war, violence or similar bad things, which are against the wellbeing of the people.

Freedom goes hand in hand with responsibility.

People can assemble peacefully only.

Question 35. Who discovered the equinoxes?

Response: **Hipparchus of Nicaea** (c. 190 BC– c. 120 BC, age c. 70, same age as Seleucus). He was a Greek astronomer, geographer, and mathematician. He is considered the founder of trigonometry, and he discovered the equinoxes.

For economy it is clear that the free market economy, while not perfect, gives the best results, but all people will have the option to choose between friendly private services, and friendly government services. Independent assistants and monitors will make sure that there are no abuses. Sine qua non requirements for happiness are morality and free market.

Italy, Venezia, Rio Ca' Foscari (left), Palazzo Balbi (center), left bank, 2.2 km from Ponte degli Scalzi

Question 36. Who explained lunar and solar eclipses?

Response: **<u>Jing Fang</u>** (78 BC – 37 BC, aged 41, born 42 years after the death of Hipparchus). He was a Chinese music theorist, mathematician and astrologer. He accurately described the basics of lunar and solar eclipses.

Religion will be free, and will help people, because usually religion promotes harmony.

The religion should be free, and is expected not to interfere with activities of the Advisors, and actually should help people.

Finland, Helsinki: a Baltic Sea canal from west to east, near Ruoholahdenpuisto, seen from a bridge on Bottenhavsgatan, near Helsinki Conservatory of Music (left).

Question 37. Who were the three great Latin poets?

Response: **<u>Publius Vergilius Maro</u>**, 15 October 70 BC in Virgilio – 21 September 19 BC, in Brindisi, aged 50 years 11 months and 6 days, 24 days before 51, 8 years younger than Jing Fang), published Georgics, Aeneid.

<u>Quintus Horatius Flaccus</u> (8 Dec 65 BC in Venosa – 27 Nov 8 BC in Rome, aged 56.9 (just 11 days before 57), 5.1 years younger than Vergilius), published Odes, Carmen Saeculare.

<u>Publius Ovidius Naso</u> (20 March 43 BC, in Sulmona – 17, in Tomis, Moesia (now Constanta, Romania, aged 60, 21.2 years younger than Horatius), published Ars Amatoria.

People of course can petition the small Word Government, and can change it anytime, if it does not perform as expected.

Italy, the entrance to the modern city of Pompei, located southeast of the ruins of the ancient Pompeii (650 BC, in 79 covered by ash).

France, Paris: Université Paris 1 Panthéon-Sorbonne (1971, after the division of the University of Paris (Sorbonne, 1150)), on Rue Saint-Jacques (left) and Rue Soufflot (right, to Panthéon (1758 – 1790)).

Question 38. Who invented the wind wheel?

Response: **Heron of Alexandria** (c. 10 AD – c. 70 AD, aged circa 60, 53 years younger than Ovidius), mathematician and engineer, who was active in his native city of Alexandria, Roman Egypt. He is considered the greatest experimenter of antiquity. Hero published a description of a steam-powered device called an aeolipile (or "Heron engine"). Among his most famous inventions was a wind wheel, constituting the earliest instance of wind harnessing on land. A wind wheel operating an organ was the first instance in history of wind powering a machine. The first vending machine was also one of his inventions, as well as automatic doors. He also wrote the earliest brief reference to square roots of negative numbers.

Without wars, Heron's wind wheel could have been developed, in over 2,000 years, to a very sophisticated machine, with many practical uses.

If there is deficit, the harmony disappears:

All budgets will have a surplus of 2% - there will be a strict application of the Latin aphorism: "Sumptus censum ne superset" (Let not your spending exceed your income). As we can see, there were good Romans telling the rulers sumptus censum ne superset, but the rulers continued to make plenty of mistakes with wars, conflicts, etc.

Question 39. Who discovered the properties of light?

Response: **<u>Claudius Ptolemaeus</u>** (c. AD 100 – c. 168, Alexandria, age c. 68, born 30 years after the death of Heron). He was a Roman mathematician, astronomer, geographer and astrologer. He lived in the city of Alexandria in the Roman province of Egypt. Ptolemaeus wrote three important scientific treatises: the first is the astronomical treatise originally entitled the *Mathematical Treatise,* the second is the *Geography*, which is a discussion of the geographic knowledge of the Greco-Roman world, and the third is the astrological treatise *Quadripartitum*. Ptolemaeus also wrote Harmonics, on music theory and the mathematics of music, following Pythagoras, 650 years after him. His book Optics includes properties of light, such as reflection, refraction, and color. Named after Ptolemaeus: the crater Ptolemaeus on the Moon; the crater Ptolemaeus on Mars; the asteroid 4001 Ptolemaeus; Ptolemaeus' theorem on distances in a cyclic quadrilateral, and its generalization, Ptolemaeus' inequality - to non-cyclic quadrilaterals; Ptolemaic graphs - the graphs whose distances satisfy Ptolemaeus' inequality.

Correcting errors is a permanent duty for everybody - Darwin (over 140 years ago, around 1880) said "To kill an error is as good a service as, and sometimes even better than, the establishing of a new truth or fact."

Question 40. What is the importance of Claudius Galenus?

Response: **Claudius Galenus**, or Galen of Pergamum (September 129, Pergamum, Mysia, Anatolia, Roman Empire (now Bergama, Turkey) – 210, Rome, Roman Empire, aged 81, 29 years younger than Ptolemaeus), Greek physician, surgeon and philosopher in the Roman Empire. His medical writings influenced the Western and Arab worlds for close to 1500 years, until circa 1700. Galenus rose from gladiators' physician in Asia Minor to court physician in the Rome of Marcus Aurelius (26 April 121, Roma, Roman Empire – 17 March 180, Vindobona, Roman Empire, aged 58.9, (8.3 years older than Galenus), called the Philosopher, Roman Emperor for 19 years, from 161 to 180).

Galenus had important medical writings, which influenced the Western and Arab worlds for close to 1500 years, until circa 1700. Without wars, his medical writings could have been very much enhanced.

Seneca (over 1,960 years ago, circa 4 BC – 65 AD, aged 69, 39 years younger than Ovidius) said "Wherever there is a human being, there is an opportunity for a kindness."

This is a fundamental idea which must be constantly applied.

Italy, Rome (753 BC): Piazza del Quirinale, with a Roman obelisk from Augustus period (27 BC – 14 AD), erected here in 1786 by Pius VII Pontifex Maximus (Supreme Pontiff), between two horse tamers to the left and right, and with a large water bowl in front, placed around 1850.

Question 41. Any idea of government mobility in 306, in Rome?

Response: No, just usual war errors - for 18 years, 306 – 324, Constantine I had wars with Maxentius, Licinius, Martinianus and others.

All levels of government will be highly mobile - changing of the capitals for the 10 regions, and for the 100 sub-regions, etc.

It is necessary to move the government close to the people, to be able to quickly solve the local problems.

Locally the people will decide how to better organize themselves, to be more efficient and harmonious, with the help of the world government when necessary. Like in any big family, there will be differences in organization and management, based on their abilities and objectives, but all must be peaceful and harmonious. Conflicts will be promptly resolved by the medical personnel, police, and other assistants.

Italy, Roma: Part of the Imperial Palaces (27 BC) on the Palatine Hill, north of the Circus Maximus (550 BC – 549 AD), the world largest stadium (250,000 people) for chariot races, for over 1,000 years.

Question 42. Who created algebra?

Response: **Diophantus of Alexandria** (211 – 295, aged 84, born 1 year after the death of Galenus). He was a mathematician, and the author of a series of books called Arithmetica, many of which are now lost because of wars and incompetence. He is called "the father of algebra", because he used symbols for unknown numbers, and wrote Arithmetica, one of the earliest treatises on algebra.

The United Nations will change in 2-3 years (for example, by 2024) into World Police and Assistance Organization (WPAO), to help local police in case of big natural disasters or big accidents, and will report to the top 10 Advisers. They will be located in all capitals, and help the locals. When an emergency appears, they will quickly move to solve the emergency.

The police powers will be limited, and they will know and be friend with all the people in their jurisdiction – this is the key element of a civilized and peaceful Earth. If they notice a person with bad intentions, they immediately retain that person and call for a medical assistant (and other assistants, if necessary), to analyze and solve the issue very quickly.

Police will be people's friends everywhere, and they will always help people.

Prevention of bad events is the main objective of everybody. If a bad event occurs, the police and their assistants will eliminate the consequences, reestablish the normal situation, and determine why the bad event occurred, in order to improve their activity, and prevent such bad events in the future.

Private property cannot be taken for public use, without just compensation, decided by at least 5 assistants.

A person cannot deprive another person of life, liberty, or property, which, unfortunately, occurs very frequently in the world, and very much effort and energy will be allocated to prevent such bad events.

In order to prevent bad things, the police, doctors and their assistants will be in permanent contact with all the people, by visiting them, phone calls, e-mails, tele-videos, and mail, to keep everybody calm and happy.

Japan, Tokyo: The small street to the east entrance to the Imperial Palace East Garden, in Tokyo, Chiyoda, with water on both sides of the street. The whole Imperial Palace complex is surrounded by water.

Question 43. Who was one of the last great Greek mathematicians of Antiquity?

Response: **Pappus of Alexandria** (c. 290 – c. 350, aged c. 60, 79 years younger than Diophantus). He was one of the last great Greek mathematicians of Antiquity, known for his Collection (c. 340, at age 50), and for Pappus's hexagon theorem in projective geometry. Collection is a compilation of mathematics in eight volumes, the bulk of which survives. It covers a wide range of topics, including geometry, recreational mathematics, doubling the cube, polygons and polyhedra.

About 66% of the people of the world are working at any moment. Therefore, non-stop working of all world government departments – especially medical, police, emergency, volunteers – will be carefully organized.

USA, Cambridge, 23 September 2009, on the campus of Harvard University (1636) in Cambridge, The Harry Elkins Widener (1885-1912 (died on Titanic)) Memorial Library (1915, Beaux-Arts architecture, 3.5 M of books).

Question 44. What is the importance of Isidore of Miletus?

Response: **<u>Isidore of Miletus</u>** (442, Miletus – 537, aged 95, born 92 years after the death of Pappus). He was a Greek mathematician, scientist and engineer, who invented, in 532, at age 90, the pendentive dome, together with Anthemius of Tralles (c. 474 – 533, aged 59, 32 years younger than Isidore). As architects, they applied the pendentive dome for the construction (532 – 537, 5 years, using ashlar and brick) of Sancta Sophia (or Sancta Sapientia, length 82 m, width 73 m, height 55 m, now it is 1,484 years old) in Constantinople, Eastern Roman Empire, on the orders of the Byzantine Emperor Justinian I, 50, (c. 482 – 14 Nov 565 (aged 83), reign for 38.2 years: 1 Aug 527 – 14 Nov 565). From the date of its construction in 537 until 1453, for 916 years, Sancta Sophia served as an Eastern Orthodox cathedral, and the seat of the Ecumenical Patriarch of Constantinople, except between 1204 and 1261, for 57 years, when it was converted by the Fourth Crusaders to a Roman Catholic cathedral under the Latin Empire. The building was later converted into an Ottoman mosque from 29 May 1453 until 1931, for 478 years. In 1919, the Divine Service in Sancta Sophia, which had been interrupted, after the Salvation, 466 years ago, in 1453, was continued and completed by a Greek military priest. It was then secularized and opened as a museum on 1 February 1935. It remained the world's largest cathedral for 983 years, until Seville Cathedral was completed in 1520.

Isidore of Miletus is important for the construction of the splendid Sancta Sophia, which is now 1,484 years old.

In order to have serious and constructive discussions and negotiations, they must be private.

Privacy and discipline are necessary for good government work.

The results will be public and preserved, but not the private discussions.

Italy, Roma: La Bocca della Verità (50 AD) is a sculpture carved from Pavonazzo marble, with a man-like face (Oceanus), located in the portico of the Basilica di Santa Maria in Cosmedin (1085).

Question 45. What is the importance of Bonifacius Secundus?

Response: – **Bonifacius Secundus** was the 55th Pope for 2 years and 25 days, until 17 Oct 532, when he died, aged 42 (48 years younger than Isidore). He was the first Germanic Pope, and, with the help of some mathematicians, at the age of 40, on 22 September 530, he changed, after 580 years, the numbering of the years in the Julian Calendar from Ab Urbe Condita (AUC, which started 1283 years ago, on 21 April 753 BC) to Anno Domini (AD, therefore AD 1 = AUC 754, AD 530 = AUC 1283, AD 1453 = AUC 2206, AD 2000 = AUC 2753, and AD 2021 = AUC 2774), which is used today, for over 1,491 years.

Bonifacius Secundus is important for this significant change in the calendar, which is used today.

It is a strict requirement for the top management, and for all others, to be highly civilized, polite, courteous, harmonious and efficient.

Who wants to work for the world government must have good manners.

Harmony in the world starts from the harmony and good manners of the people in the world government.

Because all people on Earth want to live in harmony right now, it will be relatively easy to implement this in one good and civilized country. This may include having small, beautiful and commonly agreed fences around properties, because good fences make good neighbors, and also helps with more privacy.

Question 46. Is Algoritmi important today?

Response: **Algoritmi** (circa 780 – c 850, in Baghdad, aged c 70, born 248 years after the death of Bonifacius). He was a Persian mathematician and scholar, who wrote works in mathematics (founder of algorithm), geography and astronomy, textbook on arithmetic (Algorithmo de Numero Indorum), which codified the various Indian numerals, and used the decimal number system. In 820, at age 40, Algoritmi published Algebrae et Alumcabola Algorithm. The Compendious Book on Calculation by Completion and Balancing, translated into Latin by Robert of Chester in 1145, over 325 years after it was written, was used for about 400 years, until the sixteenth century, as a mathematical text-book of European universities.

Algoritmi, as the name suggests, introduced the algorithm, which is intensely used today by all computers.

The medical personnel and others will work diligently to make sure that disputes are resolved, and then a friendship is developed. Only in this way the situation will become stable.

People want peace, freedom, health, friendship and prosperity, therefore conflicts should be quickly resolved, and then the corrective medical treatment will include the transformation of hostility and aggressiveness into harmony and friendship.

Dispute resolution is not only Government's obligation, but it will be everybody's duty.

There will be professional assistance from medical personnel, police, people assistance specialists, volunteers, religious organizations, and many others, but the bottom line is that everybody must avoid disputes.

When there are different opinions, just stay calm, express your opinion, listen to others, and continue calm the discussion until a compromise is reached.

There is no need to spend much time and energy – let the people decide, and even if your idea is not temporarily accepted, there are chances that in the future you'll have more people agree with you.

UK, London, at the east end of Westminster Bridge (1862, 250 m, width 26 m, 7 spans, right) over Thames (flowing left to right), Palace of Westminster (1016, 1870, 300 m river front façade, 1,100 rooms, center left, with Victoria Tower (1858, 98 m, left), and Central Tower (91 m)), Big Ben (Elizabeth Tower, 1855, 96 m, center right).

Question 47. Why is Avicenna important?

Response: **Avicenna** (22 August 980, in Samanid Empire (now Uzbekistan) – 21 June 1037, in Kakuyid Emirate (now Iran), aged 56.8, born 130 years after the death of Algoritmi). He was a Persian polymath, who is regarded as one of the most significant physicians, astronomers, thinkers and writers of that period. Avicenna is important because in 1025, at age 45, he published the Canon of Medicine, which set the standard for medical textbook for over 700 years, through 18th century, in Europe. After 948 years, in 1973, Avicenna's Canon of Medicine was reprinted in New York.

As a single big, over 7.7 B family on Earth, all people must be able to communicate easily with each other.

For this reason, a common language and alphabet on Earth are needed. Because English is a de facto common language now, it will be taken as the basis of the world language, let's call it Mundo, which will be taught in all schools, and used in the world government. All the other languages will continue as secondary languages.

The same is true for the Latin alphabet, which will be used everywhere, with other alphabets as secondary.

The teachers will have a very significant role in implementing this idea.

USA< New York: On W 42nd St, at Broadway, looking southeast, with Hilton Garden Inn (right, in a classic red building), and Times Square to the left.

Question 48. Why is Omar Khayyam famous?

Response: **<u>Omar Khayyam</u>** (18 May 1048 – 4 December 1131, aged 83.5, born 11.1 years after the death of Avicenna). He was a Persian mathematician, astronomer, and poet. In 1070, at age 22, he begins to write Treatise on Demonstration of Problems of Algebra, and classifies cubic equations. In 1100, he, 52, gave a complete classification of cubic equations with geometric solutions found by means of intersecting conic sections.

Omar Khayyam is famous for his mathematical results and for his beautiful poems.

The 2018 Global Wealth Report from Credit Suisse shows that the total global wealth has reached $317 trillions (circa $41,000/person), which is encouraging, and all this wealth must be used only for peace.

Like in any big family, there are differences, because some work more, some spend less, some move faster, and, especially, some are sick – this is the main reason for differences: not all people can be equally sick, some people are sicker than others. However, all the people and the government will work to help each other.

It is a major responsibility of the Government to increase the global wealth, and to train those in need, to have better working abilities and opportunities.

Italy, 12 May 1978, Bologna (1000 BC, 140 km^2, elevation 54 m, metro population 1 M, the capital and largest city of the Emilia-Romagna region in Northern Italy, with the oldest university in the world, University of Bologna, founded in 1088), west of Piazza di Porta San Donato, from Via Zamboni looking east to the north façade of the Università degli Studi di Bologna, Dipartimento di Matematica, Istituto di Matematica.

Question 49. Which is the oldest University?

Response: The University of Bologna, Italy, was founded in 1088 (when Omar Khayyam was 40 years old), and is the oldest university in continuous operation, for 933 years.

No bureaucracy – this is required by all people, and every day attention will be given for improvements in this direction.

In a well-organized country, with all people working together in harmony, this can be accomplished in several years.

Constant attention will be focused on avoiding duplication at all levels of the world government – there must be continuous collaboration between all levels, to prevent duplication, and to eliminate it, if it was found.
A vice is nourished by being concealed (from Latin: Alitur vitium vivitque tegendo).

Question 50. Is Fibonacci important?

Response: **Leonardo Bonacci** (or Leonardo di Pisa), nicknamed after 663 years, in 1838, **Fibonacci** (circa 1175- c. 1250, aged c. 75, born 87 years after the University of Bologna, Italy, was founded). The name Fibonacci comes from filius Bonacci (son of Bonacci). He was an Italian mathematician from the Republic of Pisa. In 1202, Fibonacci, 27, published his book Liber Abaci (Book of Calculation - important book on arithmetic, using Hindu-Arabic numeral system, which is used today).

Sure, his mathematical results are frequently used today, inclusive in computers.

Everybody will work really hard to completely eliminate corruption, organized crime, cybercrime and drug trafficking.

6 April 1978, Pisa, Cattedrale di Pisa (1092, striped-marble, left), Torre di Pisa (August 1173-1372, 55.86 m on the low side, 56.67 m on the high side, white-marble, 296 steps, right

Question 51. In addition to his well-known paintings, what Uccello did?

Response: **Paolo Uccello** (1397 – 10 December 1475, aged 78, born Paolo di Dono, 147 years after the death of Fibonacci). He was a famous Italian painter and mathematician, who is remembered for his pioneering work on visual perspective in art.

Each government department will have some reserves for special situations (natural disasters, big accidents), and the banks will also have good financial reserves.

All people will be encouraged to save some money in banks with 5% interest.

Italy, Rome (753 BC), the northwest side of Amphitheatrum Flavium (80, started by Flavius Vespasian (born 9 AD, emperor 69-79) in 70, and completed by his son Titus Flavius Vespasianus (born 39, emperor 79-81) in 80, wrongly called Colosseum).

Question 52. Who introduced printing to Europe?

Response: **Johannes Gensfleisch zur Laden zum Gutenberg (**1398 – 3 February 1468, aged 69, 1 year younger than Uccello), known as Gutenberg, German blacksmith, goldsmith, printer, and publisher, who introduced printing to Europe with the printing press, in 1439, at age 41, in Mainz, Holy Roman Empire, now Germany.

Inspectors will help the Government with the integrity and efficiency issues – always there are ways to improve the work.

Inspectors will give advice regarding integrity and efficiency, and will take corrective actions when necessary.

Paris (250 BC): l'Hôtel de Ville (City Hall since 1357, King Francis I started this building in 1533, finished 1628, 1873-1892

Question 53. Who is another painter and mathematician?

Response: **<u>Piero della Francesca</u>** (c. 1415 – 1492, aged 77, 17 years younger than Gutenberg). He was an Italian painter and mathematician. His painting is characterized by its serene humanism, its use of geometric forms and perspective. His most famous work is the cycle of frescoes The History of the True Cross in the church of San Francesco in the Tuscan town of Arezzo. Piero della Francesca had made a detailed study of perspective, and was the first painter to make a scientific study of light. These studies and Alberti's treatise De Pictura were to have a profound effect on younger artists, and in particular on Leonardo da Vinci's own observations and artworks.

Because all families need assistance from time to time, and the big 7.7 B family on Earth contains billions of small families, all of them will have the assistance they need – this will be the result of one country well organized and managed.

Question 54. What is Leonardo remembered for?

Response: **Leonardo da Vinci** (full name Leonardo di ser Piero da Vinci, 15 April 1452, Anchiano near Vinci (25 km west of Florence, on a Tuscan hill, in the lower valley of the Arno River), Republic of Florence (ruled by de Medici) – 2 May 1519, Amboise, Kingdom of France, aged 67 years and 17 days, 37 years younger than Piero della Francesca). He was an Italian polymath whose areas of interest included invention, painting, sculpting, architecture, science, music, mathematics, engineering, literature, anatomy, geology, astronomy, optics, botany, hydrodynamics, writing, history, and cartography, but he did not publish his findings. He is the father of paleontology, ichnology, and architecture, and is one of the greatest painters of all time. In 1487, Leonardo da Vinci, 35, drew L'Uomo Vitruviano (the Vitruvian Man, now at Accademia in Venice), which is regarded as a cultural icon, being reproduced on the euro coin, textbooks, etc. Vitruvius was an ancient Roman architect, interested in the proportions of the human body. In 1489 Leonardo da Vinci, 37, dissected for anatomical research, and he also painted Lady with an Ermine, the lady being Cecilia Gallerani – finished by 1490. In 1510, Leonardo, 58, collaborated with Professor doctor Marcantonio della Torre, 29, on his work of theoretical anatomy – until 1511, when Marcantonio della Torre died at the very young age of 30. In 1508 Leonardo da Vinci, 56, illustrated the concept of contact lenses.

Special attention will be given by Advisors to avoid abuses and wrong interpretations of the rules. All assistants (doctors, mathematicians, CEOs, engineers and teachers) will closely monitor all activities, to avoid abuses and wrong interpretations of the rules.

This requirement of not having abuses is demanding – but this is a general job, not only for Government, but for everybody, as part of the big family, we just don't need abuses.

The abuse, in some places, of confiscating the land by some government bureaucrats will be eliminated – the land belongs to the people, not the government.

The abuse, in some places, of having trains, airplanes, and others making unhealthy noises, with the government support, will be eliminated – peoples' health has always priority.

The abuse, in some places, of having to change the clocks twice a year will be eliminated – only the normal local time zones will be used.

If abuses are observed, they will be immediately reported to the Government, and corrected, in general, by the People Assistance Department, which will have personnel, including medical assistants, to analyze and promptly solve the abuses.

Paris: Rue Soufflot (from Panthéon, looking north-west to Jardin du Luxembourg (1612, back), and Tour Eiffel (1889, 324 m)), with the Université Paris 1 Panthéon-Sorbonne (1150, 1971, right).

Question 55. What is Copernicus' contribution?

Response: **Nicolaus Copernicus** (19 February 1473 – 24 May 1543, aged 70.2, 20.9 younger than Leonardo da Vinci), was a mathematician, astronomer and economist, who formulated a model of the universe that placed the Sun, rather than the Earth, at the center of the universe, independently of Aristarchus of Samos (310 BC – 230 BC), who had formulated such a model some 1780 years earlier, but the wars blocked everything. The publication of Copernicus' model in his book De revolutionibus orbium coelestium (On the Revolutions of the Celestial Spheres), just before his death in 1543, was a major event in the history of science.

In one country, with one market, the commerce between the people on Earth will be free of taxes, tariffs, duties, etc. – plenty of opportunities for everybody.

Italy, Rome: John Cabot University (1972), American University in Rome.

Question 56. Who invented the term Atlas?

Response: **<u>Gerardus Mercator</u>** (5 March 1512 – 2 December 1594, aged 82.6, 39 years younger than Copernicus). He was a Southern Dutch (current day Belgium) cartographer, geographer, mathematician and cosmographer. He was renowned for creating the 1569 (age 57) world map, based on a cylindrical projection (Mercator projection), which represented sailing courses of constant bearing (rhumb lines) as straight lines—an innovation that is still used in nautical charts. He also invented the term Atlas. He had six children.

The speech will be free and responsible. It is expected not to call for war, violence, or similar destructive activities. People want peace, freedom, health, friendship, harmony and prosperity for all.

USA, Washington, D.C. (1790): a vending cart near the east side of the Smithsonian Institution Building (1849-1855), on Jefferson Drive SW, close to 7th Street SW.

Question 57. Who is the founder of modern human anatomy?

Response: **Andreas Vesalius** (Flemish Andries Van Wesel, 31 Dec 1514, Brussels, Habsburg Netherlands – 15 Oct 1564, Zakynthos Island, Greece, aged 49.8, 2.6 years younger than Mercator), Flemish anatomist, physician, and author, in 1543 (age 29), of one of the most influential books on human anatomy, "De humani corporis fabrica libri septem". Vesalius is the founder of modern human anatomy.

The press will be free and responsible. It is expected not to call for war, violence, or similar destructive activities. People want peace, freedom, health, friendship, harmony and prosperity.

Finland, Helsinki: a commercial harbor in the south-west of the city, near Hietalahdenranta, with the boat Aranda.

Question 58. Who was first to use the term "electricity"?

Response: **William Gilbert** (24 May 1544 – 30 November 1603, aged 59.5, 29.3 years younger than Vesalius). He was an English physician, physicist and natural philosopher, who wrote the book *De Magnete* (On Magnetism, 1600, age 56), and used the term "electricity". A unit of magnetomotive force, also known as magnetic potential, was named the *Gilbert* in his honor.

People can assemble peacefully only, with police for help. It is expected not to call for war, violence, or similar destructive activities. People want peace, freedom, health, friendship, harmony and prosperity for all.

USA, New York: W 42nd Street, near 8th Avenue, with the Chrysler Building (1930, 320 m, 77 floors, center-right far back).

Question 59. Who was Iordanus Brunus Nolanus?

Response: **<u>Giordano Bruno</u>** (Latin: Iordanus Brunus Nolanus; 1548 – 17 February 1600, aged 51, born Filippo Bruno, 4 years younger than Gilbert) was an Italian mathematician, Dominican friar, philosopher, poet, and cosmological theorist, who extended the Copernican idea of a heliocentric universe (opposed to his own church's teachings). He also correctly believed in an infinite universe with numerous inhabited worlds, and was an extremely courageous philosopher.

There will always be plenty of jobs at world minimum wage (assisting other people, for example), and the standard situation will be this: more jobs than available people, so people will choose the jobs they like the most.

The city Niagara Falls, Ontario, Canada, with its Skylon Tower (center-left, 1965, 160 m, a Revolving Dining Room), and the boarding place (center-right) for the boat to the Horseshoe Falls.

France, Paris: The monument "Flamme de la Liberté" (1987, 3.5 m in height, a full-sized, gold-leaf-covered replica of the new flame at the upper end of the torch carried in the hand of the Statue of Liberty, New York), in Place de l'Alma, near the Pont de l'Alma, Paris.

Question 60. Who invented the telescope and the microscope?

Response: **<u>Galileo Galilei</u>** (15 February 1564 – 8 January 1642, aged 77.9, 16 years younger than Bruno), Italian polymath. Known for his work as mathematician, astronomer, physicist, engineer, and philosopher, Galileo has been called the "father of observational astronomy", the "father of modern physics", the "father of the scientific method", and the "father of science". In 1583, Galilei, 19, identified the constant swing of a pendulum, leading to development of reliable timekeepers. He invented in 1593, at age 29, the thermometer, then the telescope and the microscope, and also created the concept of the pendulum clock in 1637, at age 73, but he did not have time to create a working model. In 1610, at age 46, he presented telescopic observations in Sidereus Nuncius. In 1638, at age 74, he discovered the laws of falling body. In 1633, Galilei, 69, arrived in Rome for his trial by the church. Galilei used the telescope for scientific observations of celestial objects. His contributions to observational astronomy include the telescopic confirmation of the phases of Venus, the discovery of the four largest satellites of Jupiter, the observation of Saturn's rings, and the analysis of sunspots.

No unemployment, no homelessness, no begging, no tipping – just all working harmoniously, having good houses, and helping each other.

Japan, Tokyo, Shinjuku. Center-left: Tokyo Opera City Tower (234 m, 54 fl, 1996); right Shinjuku Mitsui Building (224 m, 55 fl, 1974),

Italy, Rome: The Arch of Constantine (315, left) and Amphitheatrum Flavium (80, Colosseum, right), from Via di San Gregorio

Question 61. Who discovered the laws of planetary motion?

Response: **Johannes Kepler** (1571 – 1630, aged 59, 7 years younger than Galilei) was a German mathematician, astronomer and philosopher, who discovered the principle of inverse squares, and its relationship with planetary orbits. In 1609, at age 38, Kepler discovered the first two laws of planetary motion, and in 1619, at age 48, the third law of planetary motion, and also discovered two of the Kepler-Poinsot polyhedra.

The Constitution of the World can be improved when over 66% of the voters agree.

Obviously, there will appear in the future many more advanced technologies, medicines, etc., which will certainly create conditions to have more harmony, more collaboration, etc.

Italy, Rome (753 BC, one of the oldest cities in Europe, called Roma Aeterna (The Eternal City) and Caput Mundi (Capital of the World)), from the Pincian Hill looking southwest: Piazza del Popolo (1822), with the Egyptian obelisk (36 m) of Sety I (1290–1279 BC) and Rameses II (1303, 1279–1213 BC) from Heliopolis, brought in 10 BC by Augustus (63 BC-14 AD) for Circus Maximus, in 1589 here. Basilica San Pietro (1506, 132 m, back).

Question 62. What calendar do we use today?

Response: **Gregorius Tertius Decimus (Gregory XIII)** (1502 – 10 April 1585, aged 83, 69 older than Kepler) was the 226th Italian Pope for 12 years and 332 days, until 10 April 1585, when he died. He reformed, after 1,042 years, the Julian calendar on 4 October 1582, and it is in use today, called Gregorian calendar, for over 439 years. The Gregorian calendar was introduced on the last day of the Julian calendar Thursday, 4 October 1582, which was followed by the first day of the Gregorian calendar, Friday, 15 October 1582. Each country adopted the Gregorian calendar at different times (Prussia 28 years later, in 1610, the British Empire, including the current U.S., 170 years later, in 1752).

The purpose for all people on Earth is to be healthy, to live in peace, freedom and harmony, to be prosperous, and to prepare to expand to the Moon, asteroids, Mars, and other places in the Universe, which can support life.

France, Paris: The Panthéon (1758 - 1790, 83 m height, mausoleum in the Latin Quarter in Paris, modeled on the Pantheon (126 AD) in Rome), seen from Rue Soufflot, near Rue Saint-Jacques.

Question 63. Who is the creator of the modern philosophy?

Response: **René Descartes** (Renatus Cartesius; adjectival form: "Cartesian"; 31 March 1596 – 11 February 1650, aged 53.9, born 10.9 years after the death of Gregorius). He was a French mathematician, philosopher, and scientist. He is the father of analytical geometry (1619, at age 23), and of modern philosophy. In 1636, he, 40, discovered the pair of amicable numbers 9,363,584 and 9,437,056. In 1637, he, 41, uses for the first time the term imaginary number. In 1641, René Descartes, 45, published Meditationes de prima philosophia (Meditations on First Philosophy). In 1643, he, 47, proves Descartes' theorem.

Important immediate objectives for everybody are:
- Reserve time for happiness.
- Use robots and automated processes, work less, and spend more time with your family.
- The weekend will be like a small vacation.
- Prevent burnout.
- Make civilized behavior and harmony everywhere is an important issue.
- Eliminate stress.
- Help friends and colleagues.
- Keep everybody relaxed, calm, friendly, patient, and happy.

.

Question 64. Who invented the mechanical calculator?

Response: **Blaise Pascal** (19 June 1623 – 19 August 1662, aged 39 years and 2 months, 27.2 years younger than Descartes), was an important French mathematician, physicist, inventor, and writer. He was a child prodigy, who was educated by his father. He invented the Pascaline or mechanical calculator in 1642, at age 21. In 1654, he, 31, and Pierre de Fermat, 47, created the theory of probability.

How to have harmony - using cordiality, having peaceful discussions, using a balanced approach to all issues, being amicable, coordinating the work in teams, being pleasant and melodic, etc.

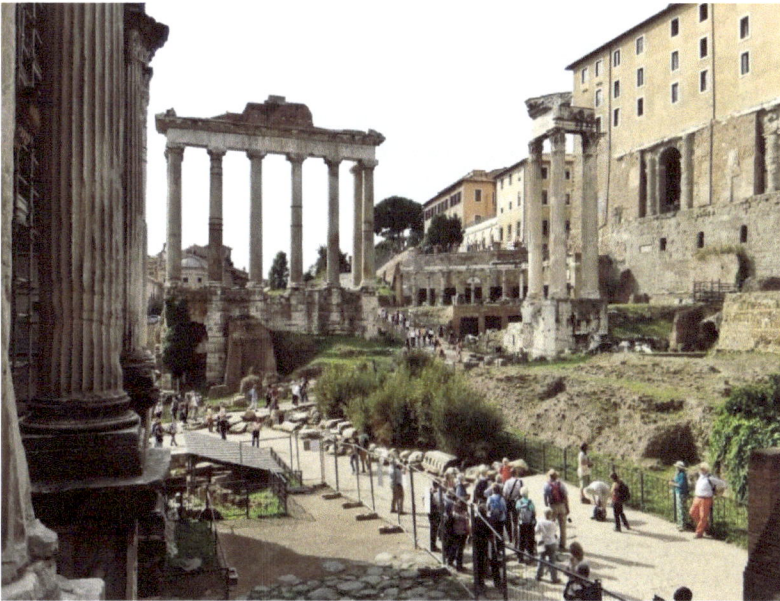

Italy, Rome (753 BC), Forum Romanum, the northwest side of Arcus Septimii Severi (left, 203, Septimius Severus (145 – 211)), the northeast part of Templum Saturni (center left, 497 BC, 42 BC, 380), Tabularium (78 BC, started by Quintus Lutatius Catulus (149 – 87 BC)) and Campidoglio right.

Question 65. Who built the first pendulum clock?

Response: **Christaan Huygens** (14 April 1629 – 8 July 1695, aged 66.2, 5.8 years younger than Pascal) was a scientist, founder of mathematical physics, had contributions in optics and mechanics, discovered Saturn's moon Titan, invented the Huygenian eyepiece for the telescope, and invented in 1656, at age 27, the pendulum clock, which was a breakthrough in timekeeping, and became the most accurate timekeeper for almost 300 years). The clock was first conceptualized 19 years before, in 1637, by Galileo Galilei, age 73, but he did not have time to create a working model. In 1680, Christaan Huygens, 51, invented the piston engine, or gunpowder engine, or explosion engine, or Huygens' engine.

For better understanding and easier implementation of this harmony and the World Constitution, the following books, by Michael M. Dediu, are recommended:
- Our Future is Sustainable Peace and Prosperity – Moving from conflicts to harmony and peace
– Our Future Depends on Good World Educations – Moving from frail education to solid education.
– Friendly, Helpful & Smart World Management - Moving from bureaucracy to responsive world management
– If You Want Peace, Prepare for Peace! – Moving from preparation for war to preparation for peace
– World with One Country & its Ten Friendly Regions - Moving from 195 disagreeing countries, to 1 country with 10 collaborating regions
– After 10,000 Years of Conflicts, People want 10,000 Years of Harmony - Moving from continuous wars to stable peace
- The Constitution of the World – Moving from many unsustainable constitutions, to just one Constitution of the World
- World Constitution Implementation – Moving from violent changes, to smooth transition to the Constitution of the World

- It is getting truer and truer – we urgently need the World Constitution: Moving from anarchic changes, to balanced transition to the Constitution of the World
- World Constitution with Lovely Comments - Moving from many suboptimal constitutions to the much better Constitution of the World

More books are listed in bibliography.

Rome: Accademia Nazionale dei Lincei (1603) in Villa Farnesina (1510). The author was invited to give a lecture here in 1977.

Question 66. Who created microbiology?

Response: **Antonie van Leeuwenhoek** (24 Oct 1632, Delft, Netherlands, - 26 August 1723, Delft, Netherlands, aged 90.8, FRS, 3.5 years younger than Huygens), Dutch businessman and scientist in the Golden Age of Dutch science and technology. A largely self-taught man in science, he is known as "the Father of Microbiology", and one of the first microscopists and microbiologists. In 1670, Antonie van Leeuwenhoek, 38, discovered blood cells, and in 1683, at age 51, he observed bacteria. Microbiology started with Antonie van Leeuwenhoek in 1676, when he was 44.

The Constitution of the World is valid not only on Earth, but also on the space around Earth, on the Moon, Mars, asteroids and any other places where the very good people on Earth will be moving in the future.

France, Paris: Rue Soufflot (left, looking north-west to Jardin du Luxembourg (1612, left back)), near Rue Saint-Jacques (right), with Université Paris 1 Panthéon-Sorbonne (right).

Question 67. Who wrote Philosophiae Naturalis Principia Mathematica?

Response: **Isaac Newton** (4 Jan 1643 – 31 March 1727, aged 84.2, 10.1 years younger than Leeuwenhoek), great English mathematician, astronomer, theologian, author and physicist. In 1665, Newton, 22, generalized binomial theorem, and began to develop a mathematical theory that later became calculus, in 1684, at age 41. In 1672, at age 29, he discovered that white light is a spectrum of a mixture of distinct colored rays. In 1675, he, 32, formulates an algorithm for the computation of functional roots. On 5 July 1687, Newton, 44.5, with encouragement and financial help from Edmond Halley, 30.75, published Philosophiae Naturalis Principia Mathematica, which laid the foundations of classical mechanics – he gave a mathematical description of the fundamental force of universal gravitation, and the three physical laws of motion.

The Constitution of the World is intended for at least 10,000 years of harmonious living on the happy Earth and many other places.

UK, London: From the southwest side of the Tower of London (left 180 m), looking south to the fortifications at the southwest corner of the third external western wall, and the City Hall (center left, after Thames).

Question 68. Who developed the binary system?

Response: **<u>Gottfried Wilhelm (von) Leibniz</u>** (1 July 1646 – 14 November 1716, aged 70.3, 3.5 years younger than Newton). He was a prominent German mathematician, and philosopher in the history of mathematics and the history of philosophy. His most notable accomplishment was conceiving the ideas of differential and integral calculus in 1684, at age 38, independently and simultaneously with Isaac Newton's, 41, similar conceptions. In 1679, at age 33, Leibniz developed the binary system, now used in all computers. In the following years Gottfried Leibniz worked on symbolic logic. In 1691, he, 45, discovered the technique of separation of variables for ordinary differential equations.

The Constitution of the World is ready to come into force, and to be put into practice, for the benefit of all people on Earth, on 6 March 2020, and it is ready to remain into force, and enjoyed by all people, at least until 6 March 12020.

Bibliography

Michael M. Dediu is also the author of these books (which can be found on Amazon.com, and www.derc.com):

1. Aphorisms and quotations – with examples and explanations
2. Axioms, aphorisms and quotations – with examples and explanations
3. 100 Great Personalities and their Quotations
4. Professor Petre P. Teodorescu – A Great Mathematician and Engineer
5. Professor Ioan Goia – A Dedicated Engineering Professor
6. Venice (Venezia) – a new perspective. A short presentation with photographs
7. La Serenissima (Venice) - a new photographic perspective. A short presentation with many photos
8. Grand Canal – Venice. A new photographic viewpoint. A short presentation with many photos
9. Piazza San Marco – Venice. A different photographic view. A short presentation with many photos
10. Roma (Rome) - La Città Eterna. A new photographic view. A short presentation with many photos
11. Why is Rome so Fascinating? A short presentation with many photos
12. Rome, Boston and Helsinki. A short photographic presentation
13. Rome and Tokyo – two captivating cities. A short photographic presentation
14. Beautiful Places on Earth – A new photographic presentation
15. From Niagara Falls to Mount Fuji via Rome - A novel photographic presentation
16. From the USA and Canada to Italy and Japan - A fresh photographic presentation
17. Paris – Why So Many Call This City Mon Amour - A lovely photographic presentation

18. The City of Light – Paris (La Ville-Lumière) - A kaleidoscopic photographic presentation
19. Paris (Lutetia Parisiorum) – the romance capital of the world - A kaleidoscopic photographic view
20. Paris and Tokyo – a joyful photographic presentation. With a preamble about the Universe

UK, London, on Thames (flowing left to right), looking northeast to the steel suspension London Millennium Footbridge (1996-2000, 325 m).

Italy, Rome (753 BC, one of the oldest continuously occupied cities in Europe, called Roma Aeterna (The Eternal City) and Caput Mundi (Capital of the World)), in Piazza Quirinale, the northeast side of Fountain of Castor (1818), with Obelisco del Quirinale (or Monte Cavallo, 1786, 29 m, from Mausoleum of Augustus (63 BC-14 AD)), and statues of the Dioscuri (Castor and Pollux, twin sons of Zeus and Leda) from the thermal baths of Constantine (272-337), Opus Phidiai on the left.

21. From USA to Japan via Canada – A cheerful photographic documentary

22. 200 Wonderful Places, In The Last 50 Years – A personal photographic documentary

23. Must see places in USA and Japan - A kaleidoscopic photographic documentary

24. Grandeurs of the World - A kaleidoscopic photographic documentary

25. Corneliu Leu – writer on the same wavelength as Mark Twain. An American viewpoint

26. From Berkeley to Pompeii via Rome – A kaleidoscopic photographic documentary

27. From America to Europe via Japan - A kaleidoscopic photographic documentary

28. Discover America and Japan - A photographic documentary

29. J. R. Lucas – philosopher on a creative parallel with Plato, An American viewpoint

30. From America to Switzerland via France - A photographic documentary

31. From Bretton Woods to New York via Cape Cod - A photographic documentary

32. Splendid Places on the Atlantic Coast of the U. S. A. - A photographic documentary

33. Fourteen nice Cities on three Continents - A photographic documentary

34. 17 Picturesque Cities on the World Map - A photographic documentary

35. Unforgettable Places from Four Continents, including Trump buildings - A photographic documentary

36. Dediu Newsletter, Volume 1, Number 1, 6 December 2016 – Monthly news, review, comments and suggestions for a better and wiser world

37. Dediu Newsletter, Volume 1, Number 2, 6 January 2017 (available also at www.derc.com).

38. Dediu Newsletter, Volume 1, Number 3, 6 February 2017 (available at www.derc.com).

39. London and Greenwich, - A photographic documentary

40. Dediu Newsletter, Volume 1, Number 4, 6 March 2017 (available also at www.derc.com).

Rome: Accademia Nazionale dei Lincei (1603, the oldest worldwide) has its library in Palazzo Corsini (1740), Via della Lungara 10, Roma.

41. Dediu Newsletter, Volume 1, Number 5, 6 April 2017 (available also at www.derc.com).
42. Dediu Newsletter, Volume 1, Number 6, 6 May 2017 (available also at www.derc.com).
43. Dediu Newsletter, Volume 1, Number 7, 6 June 2017 (available also at www.derc.com).
44. London, Oxford and Cambridge, A photographic documentary
45. Dediu Newsletter, Volume 1, Number 8, 6 July 2017 (available also at www.derc.com).
46. Dediu Newsletter, Volume 1, Number 9, 6 August 2017 (available also at www.derc.com).
47. Dediu Newsletter, Volume 1, Number 10, 6 September 2017 (available also at www.derc.com).
48. Three Great Professors: President Woodrow Wilson, Historian German Arciniegas, and Mathematician Gheorghe Vranceanu – A chronological and photographic documentary
49. Dediu Newsletter, Volume 1, Number 11, 6 October 2017 (available also at www.derc.com).
50. Dediu Newsletter, Volume 1, Number 12, 6 November 2017 (available also at www.derc.com).
51. Dediu Newsletter, Volume 2, Number 1 (13), 6 December 2017 (available also at www.derc.com).
52. Two Great Leaders: Augustus and George Washington - A chronological and photographic documentary
53. Dediu Newsletter, Volume 2, Number 2 (14), 6 January 2018 (available also at www.derc.com).
54. Newton, Benjamin Franklin, and Gauss, A chronological and photographic documentary
55. Dediu Newsletter, Volume 2, Number 3 (15), 6 February 2018 (available also at www.derc.com).
56. 2017: World Top Events, But Many Little Known, A chronological and photographic documentary
57. Dediu Newsletter, Volume 2, Number 4 (16), 6 March 2018 (available also at www.derc.com).
58. Vergilius, Horatius, Ovidius, and Shakespeare - A chronological and photographic documentary.
59. Dediu Newsletter, Volume 2, Number 5 (17), 6 April 2018 (available also at www.derc.com).

USA, Boston: a view of the north-east part of Boston, from Cambridge, over Charles River Basin. Federal Reserve Bank Building (187 m, left), and other tall buildings in the financial district.

60. Dediu Newsletter, Volume 2, Number 6 (18), 6 May 2018 (available also at www.derc.com).

61. Vivaldi, Bach, Mozart, and Verdi - A chronological and photographic documentary.

62. Dediu Newsletter, Volume 2, Number 7 (19), 6 June 2018 (available also at www.derc.com).

63. Dediu Newsletter, Volume 2, Number 8 (20), 6 July 2018 (available also at www.derc.com).

64. Dediu Newsletter, Volume 2, Number 9 (21), 6 August 2018 (available also at www.derc.com).

65. World History, a new perspective - A chronological and photographic documentary.

66. World Humor History with over 100 Jokes, a new perspective - A chronological and photographic documentary

67. Dediu Newsletter, Volume 2, Number 10 (22), 6 September 2018 (available also at www.derc.com).

68. Dediu Newsletter, Volume 2, Number 11 (23), 6 October 2018 (available also at www.derc.com).

69. Dediu Newsletter, Volume 2, Number 12 (24), 6 November 2018

70. Da Vinci, Michelangelo, Rembrandt, Rodin - A chronological and photographic documentary

71. Dediu Newsletter, Volume 3, Number 1 (25), 6 December 2018

72. Dediu Newsletter, Volume 3, Number 2 (26), 6 January 2019

73. From Euclid to Edison – revelries in the past 75 years - A chronological and photographic documentary

74. – Socrates to Churchill Aphorisms celebrated after 1960 - A chronological and photographic documentary

75. - Dediu Newsletter, Volume 3, Number 3 (27), 6 February 2019

76. – Hippocrates to Fleming: Medicine History celebrated after 1943 - A chronological and photographic documentary

77. - Dediu Newsletter, Volume 3, Number 4 (28), 6 March 2019

78. - Dediu Newsletter, Volume 3, Number 5 (29), 6 April 2019

79 – Archimedes to Ford: Invention History celebrated after 1943 - A chronological and photographic documentary

80 - Dediu Newsletter, Volume 3, Number 6 (30), 6 May 2019

81 – Sutherland to Pavarotti: Great Singers History - A chronological and photographic documentary

82 - Dediu Newsletter, Volume 3, Number 7 (31), 6 June 2019

A south-west view of Rome from Altare della Patria: Theatrum
Marcelli (the Theatre of Marcellus (Marcus Claudius Marcellus, 42
BC – 23 BC, Emperor Augustus' nephew), 13 BC, left back).

83 - Dediu Newsletter, Volume 3, Number 8 (32), 6 July 2019
84 – Augustus to Rockefeller: History of the Wealthiest People - A chronological and photographic documentary
85 - Dediu Newsletter, Volume 3, Number 9 (33), 6 August 2019
86 – Pythagoras to Fermi: History of Science - A chronological and photographic documentary
87 - Dediu Newsletter, Volume 3, Number 10 (34), 6 September 2019
88 – Our Future is Sustainable Peace and Prosperity – Moving from conflicts to harmony and peace
89 - Dediu Newsletter, Volume 3, Number 11 (35), 6 October 2019 – World Monthly Report with news
90 – Our Future Depends on Good World Educations – Moving from frail education to solid education
91 - Dediu Newsletter, Volume 3, Number 12 (36), 6 November 2019 – World Monthly Report with News and Suggestions for Sustainable Peace, Freedom and Prosperity
92 – Friendly, Helpful & Smart World Management - Moving from bureaucracy to responsive world management
93 – If You Want Peace, Prepare for Peace! – Moving from preparation for war to preparation for peace
94 - Dediu Newsletter, Volume 4, Number 1 (37), 6 December 2019 – World Monthly Report with News and Suggestions for Sustainable Peace, Freedom and Prosperity
95 – World with One Country & its Ten Friendly Regions - Moving from 195 disagreeing countries, to 1 country with 10 collaborating regions
96 - Dediu Newsletter, Volume 4, Number 2 (38), 6 January 2020 – World Monthly Report with News and Suggestions for Sustainable Peace, Freedom and Prosperity
97 – After 10,000 Years of Conflicts, People want 10,000 Years of Harmony - Moving from continuous wars to stable peace
98 - Dediu Newsletter, Volume 4, Number 3 (39), 6 February 2020 – World Monthly Report with News and Suggestions for Sustainable Peace, Freedom and Prosperity
99 – The Constitution of the World – Moving from many unsustainable constitutions, to just one Constitution of the World

Paris (founded circa 250 BC): L'Hôtel National des Invalides (1678), in the 7th arrondissement, with military museums (including details about Lafayette) and monuments, and the burial site for Napoleon Bonaparte, 1769-1821, 52.

100 - Dediu Newsletter, Volume 4, Number 4 (40), 6 March 2020 –
World Monthly Report with News and Suggestions for Sustainable
Peace, Freedom and Prosperity

101 - Dediu Newsletter, Volume 4, Number 5 (41), 6 April 2020 –
World Monthly Report

102 - Dediu Newsletter, Volume 4, Number 6 (42), 6 May 2020 –
World Monthly Report

103 – World Constitution Implementation – Moving from violent
changes, to smooth transition to the Constitution of the World

104 - Dediu Newsletter, Volume 4, Number 7 (43), 6 June 2020 –
World Monthly Report

105 - Dediu Newsletter, Volume 4, Number 8 (44), 6 July 2020 –
World Monthly Report

106 - It is getting truer and truer – we urgently need the World
Constitution: Moving from anarchic changes, to balanced transition
to the Constitution of the World

107 - Dediu Newsletter, Volume 4, Number 9 (45), 6 August 2020
– World Monthly Report

108 - World Constitution with Lovely Comments - Moving from
many suboptimal constitutions to the much better Constitution of the
World

109 - Dediu Newsletter, Volume 4, Number 10 (46), 6 September
2020 – World Monthly Report

110 – World Constitution with Questions & Answers – Moving
from many obsolete constitutions to the much better Constitution of
the World

111 - Dediu Newsletter, Volume 4, Number 11 (47), 6 October 2020
– World Monthly Report

112 - World Projects - Moving from minor projects to great projects
for the World

113 - Dediu Newsletter, Volume 4, Number 12 (48), 6 November
2020 – World Monthly Report

114 - Dediu Newsletter, Volume 5, Number 1 (49), 6 December
2020 – World Monthly Report

115 - World Opportunities for All - Moving from few local jobs, to
world opportunities for all

116 - Dediu Newsletter, Volume 5, Number 2 (50), 6 January 2021
– World Monthly Report

USA, New York: On Broadway at 43rd St, looking southwest, in Times Square

117 - Self-Managing World - Moving from local ruling top-down, to self-managing world

118 – We are all in the same space boat – Peaceful Terra; Moving from local fragile boats to the solid Peaceful Terra

119 - Dediu Newsletter, Volume 5, Number 3 (51), 6 February 2021 – World Monthly Report

120 - All people ask for Peace + Freedom = Prosperity, Moving from local conflicts to world peace and freedom

121 - Dediu Newsletter, Volume 5, Number 4 (52), 6 March 2021 – World Monthly Report

122 - To pour Peace from a cup full of arms, MELT ALL ARMS! - Moving from arms race, to peace enjoyment

123 - Dediu Newsletter Vol 5, Number 5 (53), 6 April 2021 – World Monthly Report

124 - Bureaucracy is growing like a weed - People want a Quality Change; Yup, that's right! Better life for all!

125 - Dediu Newsletter Vol 5, Number 6 (54), 6 May 2021

126 – What is Life for Homo Sapiens post 2020? – Life is evolution by harmony, not by natural selection for people.

127 - Dediu Newsletter Vol 5, Number 7 (55), 6 June 2021 – World Monthly Report

128 – All Wars and Conflicts are due to HUMAN ERRORS: Moving from perpetual war errors, to friendly collaboration and peace

129 - Dediu Newsletter Vol 5, Number 8 (56), 6 July 2021 - World Monthly Report

Italy, Venezia - The south of La Piazzetta, the south of Piazza San Marco, with gondole, and wedding pictures of a Japanese couple.

USA, New York (1624): on Broadway, close to Times Square, and to Times Square Tower (2004, 221 m, 47 floors).

www.ingramcontent.com/pod-product-compliance
Lightning Source LLC
Chambersburg PA
CBHW041308210326
41599CB00003B/25